DIABETICS AIR FRYER COOKBOOK

The Complete Guide to Preparing Easy, Healthy & Mouthwatering, Diabetes-Friendly Air Fryer Meals in Minutes. 4 Weeks Meal Plan

ALINA SMITH

Copyright © 2024 By **ALINA SMITH**. All rights reserved worldwide.

No part of this book may be reproduced or transmitted in any form or by any means, electronic or mechanical, including photocopying, recording, or by any information storage and retrieval system, without written permission from the publisher, except for the inclusion of brief quotations in a review.

Warning Disclaimer:
The purpose of this book is to educate and entertain. The author or publisher does not guarantee that anyone following the techniques, suggestions, tips, ideas, or strategies will become successful. The author and publisher shall have neither liability nor responsibility to anyone with respect to any loss or damage caused, or alleged to be caused, directly or indirectly, by the information contained in this book.

This copyright notice and disclaimer apply to the entirety of the book and its contents, whether in print or electronic form, and extend to all future editions or revisions of the book. Unauthorized use or reproduction of this book or its contents is strictly prohibited and may result in legal action

TABLE OF CONTENTS

- 4-WEEKS MEAL PLAN 6
- INTRODUCTION TO DIABETES AND AIR FRYING 8
  - BENEFITS OF AIR FRYING FOR DIABETICS 8
  - TIPS FOR HEALTHY COOKING AND EATING WITH DIABETES 9
- CHAPTER 1: GETTING STARTED WITH AIR FRYING 10
  - ESSENTIAL TOOLS AND INGREDIENTS FOR DIABETIC FRIENDLY AIR FRYING 10
  - SAFETY PRECAUTIONS AND MAINTENANCE TIPS 11
- CHAPTER 2: BREAKFAST DELIGHTS 13
  - Avocado Toast with Egg 13
  - Spinach and Feta Frittata 13
  - WholeGrain Banana Bread 14
  - Cinnamon Sugar Doughnuts 15
  - Sweet Potato Hash 16
  - Blueberry Oatmeal Cups 17
  - VeggiePacked Breakfast Burrito 18
  - Zucchini Bread 19
  - Protein Packed Granola 20
  - Egg Muffins with Vegetables 21
  - Greek Yogurt Parfait with Berries 21
  - Savory Oatmeal with Mushrooms and Spinach 22
  - Whole Wheat Pancakes 22
  - Overnight Chia Pudding 23
  - Breakfast Cauliflower Rice Bowls 24
- CHAPTER 3: APPETIZERS AND SNACKS 25
  - Crispy Chickpeas 25
  - Zucchini Fries 26
  - Garlic Parmesan Kale Chips 27
  - Avocado Fries 28
  - Baked Sweet Potato Chips 29
  - Cauliflower Buffalo Wings 30
  - Cucumber Bites with Tzatziki 31
  - Roasted Edamame 32
  - Baked Avocado Boats 33
  - Roasted Beet Hummus 34
  - AirFried Deviled Eggs 35
  - Crispy Tofu Bites 36
  - AirFried Falafel 37
  - Caprese Skewers 38
  - Sweet and Spicy Nuts 38
- CHAPTER 4: SOUPS AND SALADS 39

2 | Diabetics Air Fryer Cookbook

Creamy Broccoli Soup 39
Lentil and Vegetable Soup 40
Tomato Basil Soup 41
Butternut Squash Soup 42
Chicken and Veggie Soup 43
Spinach Salad with Warm Bacon Dressing 44
Greek Salad 45
Quinoa and Black Bean Salad 46
Kale and Brussels Sprouts Salad 47
Cobb Salad 48
Taco Salad 49
Caprese Salad 50
Arugula Salad with Roasted Beets 51
Southwest Chicken Salad 52
LemonHerb Chicken Salad 53

CHAPTER 5: VEGETARIAN MAINS 54

Cauliflower Steaks with Chimichurri Sauce 54
Stuffed Portobello Mushrooms 55
Vegetable Frittata 56
Lentil and Sweet Potato Shepherd's Pie 57
QuinoaStuffed Bell Peppers 58
Veggie Burgers 59
Tofu StirFry 60
Eggplant Parmesan 61
Zucchini Lasagna 62
Chickpea Curry 63
Vegetable Enchiladas 64
Sweet Potato and Black Bean Burrito Bowls 65
Roasted Vegetable Medley 66
Vegetarian Chili 67
Baked Falafel with Tzatziki Sauce 68

CHAPTER 6: POULTRY AND SEAFOOD 69

Cauliflower Steaks with Chimichurri Sauce 69
Stuffed Portobello Mushrooms 70
Vegetable Frittata 71
Lentil and Sweet Potato Shepherd's Pie 72
QuinoaStuffed Bell Peppers 73
Veggie Burgers 74
Tofu StirFry 75
Eggplant Parmesan 76
Zucchini Lasagna 77
Chickpea Curry 78
Vegetable Enchiladas 79
Sweet Potato and Black Bean Burrito Bowls 80
Roasted Vegetable Medley 81
Vegetarian Chili 82

Baked Falafel with Tzatziki Sauce 83

CHAPTER 7: BEEF AND PORK 84

Beef and Vegetable Kebabs 84
Pork Chops with Apple Compote 85
Meatballs with Marinara Sauce 86
Beef Fajitas 87
Pork Tenderloin with Roasted Vegetables 88
Beef Meatloaf 89
Pulled Pork Sandwiches 90
Beef Burgers with Caramelized Onions 91
Pork Carnitas 92
Beef Stroganoff 93
Pork Chops with Mushroom Gravy 94
Salisbury Steak 95
Beef Enchiladas 96
Pork Chili Verde 97
Meatball Subs 98

CHAPTER 8: SIDE DISHES 99

Roasted Brussels Sprouts 99
Mashed Cauliflower 99
AirFried Asparagus 100
Roasted Sweet Potato Wedges 100
Garlic Parmesan Zucchini Noodles 101
Crispy Roasted Potatoes 102
AirFried Green Beans 102
Cauliflower Rice Pilaf 103
Broccoli and Cheddar Fritters 103
AirFried Eggplant with Marinara 104
Loaded Mashed Cauliflower 105
Roasted Carrots with HoneyMustard Glaze 106
Zucchini Fritters 107

CHAPTER 9: BREADS AND BAKED GOODS 108

WholeWheat Dinner Rolls 108
AirFried Bagels 109
Zucchini Bread 110
Banana Bread 111
Pumpkin Bread 112
WholeWheat Pizza Crust 113
AirFried Biscuits 114
Cornbread 115
AirFried Donuts 116
WholeWheat Tortillas 117
Garlic Knots 118
Prep: 20 mins | Cook: 12 mins | Serves: 6 rolls 119
WholeWheat Waffles 120

4 | Diabetics Air Fryer Cookbook

WholeGrain Muffins 121
AirFried Pretzels 122

CHAPTER 10: DESSERTS 123

Baked Apples 123
AirFried Churros 124
Chocolate Avocado Mousse 125
Raspberry Parfaits 125
Lemon Bars 126
Peanut Butter Cups 127
Coconut Macaroons 128
AirFried Fruit Crisps 129
Dark Chocolate Bark 130
Pumpkin Spice Squares 131
Almond Flour Brownies 132
Strawberry Chia Pudding 133
Baked Pears with Honey and Walnuts 133
Coconut Flour Cookies 134
Carrot Cake Cupcakes 135

CHAPTER 11: BEVERAGES 136

Fresh Fruit Smoothies 136
Iced Herbal Teas 136
Infused Waters 137
Hot Chocolate (Sugarfree) 137
Iced Coffee (Unsweetened) 138
Vegetable Juices 138
Golden Milk (Turmeric Latte) 139
Matcha Latte 139
Ginger Tea 140
Chia Fresca 140
Kombucha 141
Kefir Smoothies 142
Cucumber Mint Water 142
Pomegranate Iced Tea 143
Beet Lemonade 143

GLOSSARY TERMS 144

VOLUME MEASUREMENTS 145

CONCLUSION 147

ENCOURAGEMENT AND PATHING WORDS 148

4-WEEKS MEAL PLAN

Week	Day	Breakfast	Lunch	Dinner
Week 1	Day 1	Avocado Toast with Egg	Lentil and Vegetable Soup	Chickpea Curry
	Day 2	Blueberry Oatmeal Cups	Spinach Salad with Warm Bacon Dressing	Cauliflower Steaks with Chimichurri Sauce
	Day 3	Whole Wheat Pancakes	Quinoa and Black Bean Salad	Beef Fajitas
	Day 4	Greek Yogurt Parfait with Berries	Kale and Brussels Sprouts Salad	Pork Chops with Apple Compote
	Day 5	Overnight Chia Pudding	Taco Salad	Vegetable Enchiladas
	Day 6	Savory Oatmeal with Mushrooms and Spinach	Cobb Salad	Meatballs with Marinara Sauce
	Day 7	Whole Grain Banana Bread	Caprese Salad	Lentil and Sweet Potato Shepherd's Pie
Week 2	Day 1	Spinach and Feta Frittata	Creamy Broccoli Soup	Vegetable Stir-Fry
	Day 2	Veggie-Packed Breakfast Burrito	Greek Salad	Zucchini Lasagna
	Day 3	Protein Packed Granola	Lentil and Vegetable Soup	Baked Falafel with Tzatziki Sauce
	Day 4	Egg Muffins with Vegetables	Quinoa and Black Bean Salad	Chickpea Curry
	Day 5	Sweet Potato Hash	Taco Salad	Beef and Vegetable Kebabs
	Day 6	Whole Wheat Pancakes	Greek Salad	Chicken and Veggie Soup
	Day 7	Blueberry Oatmeal Cups	Kale and Brussels Sprouts Salad	Pork Tenderloin with Roasted Vegetables
Week 3	Day 1	Zucchini Bread	Tomato Basil Soup	Cauliflower Steaks with Chimichurri Sauce
	Day 2	Cinnamon Sugar Doughnuts	Lentil and Vegetable Soup	Beef Burgers with Caramelized Onions
	Day 3	Greek Yogurt Parfait with Berries	Quinoa and Black Bean Salad	Eggplant Parmesan
	Day 4	Avocado Toast with Egg	Taco Salad	Pork Chili Verde

Week	Day	Breakfast	Lunch	Dinner
	Day 5	Protein Packed Granola	Greek Salad	Beef Enchiladas
	Day 6	Spinach and Feta Frittata	Cobb Salad	Pulled Pork Sandwiches
	Day 7	Overnight Chia Pudding	Kale and Brussels Sprouts Salad	Salisbury Steak
Week 4	Day 1	WholeGrain Banana Bread	Creamy Broccoli Soup	Vegetable Frittata
	Day 2	Sweet Potato Hash	Lentil and Vegetable Soup	Zucchini Lasagna
	Day 3	Blueberry Oatmeal Cups	Quinoa and Black Bean Salad	Baked Falafel with Tzatziki Sauce
	Day 4	Avocado Toast with Egg	Taco Salad	Chickpea Curry
	Day 5	Protein Packed Granola	Greek Salad	Beef and Vegetable Kebabs
	Day 6	Whole Wheat Pancakes	Kale and Brussels Sprouts Salad	Chicken and Veggie Soup
	Day 7	VeggiePacked Breakfast Burrito	Caprese Salad	Pork Tenderloin with Roasted Vegetables

This meal plan offers a variety of breakfast, lunch, and dinner diet plan. Adjust servings and recipes as needed to suit personal preferences and dietary requirements.

INTRODUCTION TO DIABETES AND AIR FRYING

Living with diabetes can be challenging, but with the right knowledge, lifestyle choices, and tools, you can manage it effectively and still enjoy delicious, satisfying meals. This cookbook is designed to help you do just that by harnessing the power of air frying - a revolutionary cooking method that allows you to create crispy, flavorful dishes with little to no oil.

Diabetes is a chronic condition that affects how your body processes glucose, the main source of fuel for your cells. There are two primary types: type 1 and type 2.

Type 1 diabetes is an autoimmune disorder where the body's immune system attacks and destroys the insulin producing cells in the pancreas. Without insulin, glucose cannot enter the cells, leading to high blood sugar levels. Type 1 diabetes is typically diagnosed in childhood or adolescence and requires lifelong insulin therapy.

Type 2 diabetes is the more common form, accounting for around 90% of cases. It occurs when the body becomes resistant to insulin or doesn't produce enough insulin to regulate blood sugar levels effectively. Type 2 diabetes is often associated with lifestyle factors such as obesity, lack of physical activity, and an unhealthy diet, although genetics can also play a role.

Both types of diabetes, if left unmanaged, can lead to serious complications such as heart disease, stroke, kidney disease, nerve damage, and vision problems. However, with proper management through a combination of medication (if prescribed), regular exercise, and a balanced, nutrientrich diet, people with diabetes can live long, healthy lives.

Common symptoms of diabetes include increased thirst and urination, fatigue, blurred vision, slowhealing cuts or bruises, and tingling or numbness in the hands or feet. If you experience any of these symptoms, it's crucial to consult your healthcare provider for proper diagnosis and treatment.

BENEFITS OF AIR FRYING FOR DIABETICS

Air frying is a gamechanger for those with diabetes who love crispy, fried foods but want to minimize their intake of unhealthy fats and calories. Here are some key benefits of air frying:

Low in Fat and Calories: Air fryers use little to no oil, significantly reducing the amount of fat and calories in your meals compared to traditional deepfrying methods.

Retains Nutrients: Unlike deepfrying, air frying doesn't involve submerging foods in hot oil, which can deplete their nutritional value. Airfried foods retain more vitamins, minerals, and antioxidants, making them a healthier choice.

Versatility: Air fryers can cook a wide variety of foods, from vegetables and proteins to baked goods and even desserts, allowing you to enjoy a diverse and satisfying diet.

Portion Control: The compact size of air fryers makes it easier to prepare smaller portions, which can help with portion control - a crucial aspect of managing diabetes and maintaining a healthy weight.

Convenience: Air fryers are easy to use, require minimal preheating time, and cook food quickly, making them a convenient option for busy lifestyles.

TIPS FOR HEALTHY COOKING AND EATING WITH DIABETES

While air frying is a healthier cooking method, it's still essential to make mindful choices when it comes to ingredients and portion sizes. Here are some tips to help you make the most of your air fryer while managing diabetes:

Focus on Whole, Nutrient Dense Foods: Fill your air fryer with a variety of fresh vegetables, lean proteins, whole grains, and healthy fats like avocado, nuts, and olive oil. These foods are packed with fiber, vitamins, minerals, and antioxidants that support overall health and can help regulate blood sugar levels.

Watch Your Portions: Even though air fried foods are lower in fat and calories, it's still important to practice portion control. Use smaller plates or bowls, and be mindful of serving sizes, especially for carbohydrate rich foods.

Balance Your Plate: Aim for a balanced meal by including a source of lean protein, a serving of complex carbohydrates (such as whole grains or starchy vegetables), and plenty of non-starchy vegetables. This combination can help keep blood sugar levels stable and provide a range of nutrients.

Experiment with Flavorings: Instead of relying on salt, sugar, or unhealthy fats for flavor, explore the use of herbs, spices, vinegar, citrus juices, and other natural flavorings. These can add depth and complexity to your dishes without compromising your health goals.

Stay Hydrated: Drinking plenty of water and other low-calorie beverages, such as unsweetened teas or infused waters, can help manage blood sugar levels and prevent dehydration, a common issue for those with diabetes.

Monitor Your Blood Sugar: Regularly checking your blood sugar levels, especially before and after meals, can help you understand how different foods and cooking methods affect your body. This information can guide you in making informed choices about what to eat and how much.

Consult Your Healthcare Team: Work closely with your healthcare provider, a certified diabetes educator, or a registered dietitian to develop a personalized meal plan that meets your specific needs and takes into account any medications you may be taking.

By combining the benefits of air frying with a balanced, nutrient rich diet and a healthy lifestyle, you can effectively manage your diabetes while enjoying delicious, satisfying meals. This cookbook is designed to provide you with a wealth of air fryer recipes that cater to your dietary needs, making it easier to stick to your goals and savor every bite.

CHAPTER 1: GETTING STARTED WITH AIR FRYING

Getting Started with Air Frying

Air frying is a revolutionary cooking method that has taken the culinary world by storm, and for good reason. It allows you to enjoy crispy, delicious foods without the guilt and health risks associated with traditional deepfrying. As someone living with diabetes, embracing air frying can be a gamechanger in your journey towards a healthier lifestyle. In this section, we'll guide you through the process of choosing the right air fryer, equipping your kitchen with essential tools and ingredients, and ensuring a safe and enjoyable air frying experience

Choosing the Right Air Fryer for Your Needs

With the growing popularity of air fryers, the market is flooded with a wide range of options, making it challenging to choose the best one for your needs. Here are some key factors to consider:

Capacity: Air fryers come in various sizes, typically ranging from 2 quarts to 6 quarts or more. Consider the size of your household and the amount of food you'll be preparing. A smaller air fryer may suffice for one or two people, while larger families or those who love batch cooking may prefer a larger capacity.

Features: Look for air fryers with adjustable temperature controls, timers, and presets for different types of foods. Some models even offer advanced features like dehydrating or rotisserie functions, which can expand your cooking possibilities.

Design: Air fryers come in various shapes, from compact and basketstyle to larger and ovenlike. Consider your counter space and storage options when choosing the design that best fits your kitchen.

Ease of Use and Cleaning: Look for air fryers with removable, dishwashersafe baskets or trays, and nonstick surfaces for easy cleaning. Userfriendly controls and clear instructions can also make your air frying experience more enjoyable.

Brand Reputation and Reviews: Research reputable brands and read reviews from other users to gauge the overall quality, performance, and durability of the air fryer you're considering.

ESSENTIAL TOOLS AND INGREDIENTS FOR DIABETIC FRIENDLY AIR FRYING

While an air fryer is the star of the show, having the right tools and ingredients on hand can elevate your air frying experience and ensure consistently delicious, diabetesfriendly meals.

Tools:

1. Silicone or Heat Resistant Utensils: Invest in a set of silicone or heatresistant utensils, such as tongs, spatulas, and whisks, to safely handle hot foods and avoid scratching the nonstick surfaces.

2. Air Fryer Accessories: Many air fryers come with additional accessories like baking pans, skewers, or racks, which can expand your cooking options. You can also purchase aftermarket accessories like multilayer racks or pizza pans for added versatility.

3. Food Thermometer: A reliable food thermometer is essential for ensuring that your proteins are cooked to a safe internal temperature, reducing the risk of foodborne illnesses.

4. Silicone Mats or Parchment Paper: These handy tools can help prevent sticking and make cleanup a breeze, especially when cooking delicate or battered foods.

Ingredients:

1. Lean Proteins: Opt for lean cuts of meat, poultry, fish, or plantbased proteins like tofu or tempeh, which are lower in saturated fat and calories.

2. Fresh Vegetables: Stock up on a variety of fresh veggies, including leafy greens, cruciferous vegetables, and colorful options like bell peppers and zucchini.

3. Whole Grains: Quinoa, brown rice, wholewheat bread or wraps, and other whole grains provide a good source of fiber and can help regulate blood sugar levels.

4. Healthy Fats: Include moderate amounts of hearthealthy fats like avocado, olive oil, nuts, and seeds in your air fryer recipes for added flavor and satiety.

5. Herbs and Spices: Build a wellstocked spice rack with a variety of dried herbs and spices to add depth of flavor without relying on excessive salt, sugar, or unhealthy fats.

6. Low Sodium Broth or Stock: Opt for low sodium broths or stocks to add moisture and flavor to your air fryer dishes without increasing your sodium intake.

SAFETY PRECAUTIONS AND MAINTENANCE TIPS

Air fryers are generally safe and easy to use, but it's important to follow some basic precautions and maintenance tips to ensure a worryfree air frying experience:

Safety Precautions:

1. Read the Manual: Carefully read and follow the manufacturer's instructions for your specific air fryer model to ensure proper operation and avoid potential hazards.
2. Keep It Stable: Place your air fryer on a level, heatresistant surface, and avoid moving it while in use to prevent spills or burns.
3. Mind the Hot Surfaces: Air fryers can get extremely hot during operation. Use oven mitts or heatresistant utensils when handling the basket or trays, and keep children and pets at a safe distance.
4. Avoid Overcrowding: Never overfill the air fryer basket or tray, as this can lead to uneven cooking, increased cooking times, and potential safety hazards.
5. Monitor Cooking: Stay in the kitchen while your air fryer is in operation, and check on your food regularly to prevent overcooking or burning.

Maintenance Tips:

1. Regular Cleaning: Keep your air fryer clean by wiping down the interior and exterior surfaces after each use. Refer to the manufacturer's instructions for proper cleaning methods and materials.
2. Descale and Deodorize: Over time, minerals from water or food particles can build up in your air fryer, affecting its performance. Follow the manufacturer's guidelines for descaling and deodorizing your unit to keep it functioning optimally.

3. Store Properly: When not in use, store your air fryer in a cool, dry place, and avoid stacking heavy items on top of it to prevent damage.
4. Replace Accessories: If your air fryer came with accessories like baskets or trays, replace them if they become worn or damaged to ensure safe and efficient operation.
5. Consider a Warranty: Some air fryer manufacturers offer extended warranties or protection plans, which can provide peace of mind and potentially save you money on repairs or replacements.

By following these guidelines and equipping your kitchen with the right tools and ingredients, you'll be well on your way to mastering the art of air frying and enjoying delicious, diabetesfriendly meals with ease. **Get ready to explore a world of crispy, flavorful dishes while prioritizing your health and managing your diabetes effectively.**

CHAPTER 2: BREAKFAST DELIGHTS

Avocado Toast with Egg

Prep: 5 mins | Cook: 10 mins | Serves: 2

Ingredients:
- 2 ripe avocados, sliced (US) / 2 ripe avocados, sliced (UK)
- 4 slices wholegrain bread (US) / 4 slices wholemeal bread (UK)
- 2 eggs
- Salt and pepper, to taste

Instructions:
1. Preheat your air fryer to 350°F (180°C) for 3 minutes. [Function used: Preheat]
2. Place the slices of bread in the air fryer basket and air fry for 5 minutes until crispy. [Function used: Air frying]
3. Mash the avocado slices with a fork and spread evenly on the toasted bread slices.
4. Create a small well in the center of each avocado toast and crack an egg into each well.
5. Season the eggs with salt and pepper.
6. Air fry for 5 minutes, or until the eggs are cooked to your desired doneness. [Function used: Air frying]
7. Serve hot and enjoy!

Nutritional Info (per serving): Calories: 300 | Fat: 20g | Carbs: 25g | Protein: 10g

Tip: Ensure your avocado slices are ripe for easier mashing and better flavor.

Spinach and Feta Frittata

Prep: 10 mins | Cook: 20 mins | Serves: 4

Ingredients:
- 6 eggs
- 1 cup fresh spinach, chopped (US) / 100g fresh spinach, chopped (UK)
- 1/2 cup crumbled feta cheese (US) / 50g crumbled feta cheese (UK)
- Salt and pepper, to taste

Instructions:
1. Preheat your air fryer to 350°F (180°C) for 3 minutes. [Function used: Preheat]
2. In a mixing bowl, whisk the eggs and season with salt and pepper.
3. Stir in the chopped spinach and crumbled feta cheese.
4. Pour the egg mixture into a greased air fryersafe baking dish.
5. Air fry for 1520 minutes, or until the frittata is set and golden brown on top. [Function used: Air frying]
6. Slice into wedges and serve warm.

Nutritional Info (per serving): Calories: 180 | Fat: 12g | Carbs: 3g | Protein: 14g

Tip: Customize your frittata by adding diced bell peppers, onions, or mushrooms for extra flavor and nutrients.

WholeGrain Banana Bread

Prep: 15 mins | Cook: 30 mins | Serves: 8 slices

Ingredients:
- ✓ 2 ripe bananas, mashed (US) / 2 ripe bananas, mashed (UK)
- ✓ 1/4 cup unsweetened applesauce (US) / 60ml unsweetened applesauce (UK)
- ✓ 1/4 cup honey (US) / 60ml honey (UK)
- ✓ 1/4 cup almond milk (US) / 60ml almond milk (UK)
- ✓ 1 teaspoon vanilla extract
- ✓ 1 cup whole wheat flour (US) / 120g wholemeal flour (UK)
- ✓ 1 teaspoon baking powder
- ✓ 1/2 teaspoon baking soda
- ✓ 1/2 teaspoon cinnamon
- ✓ Pinch of salt

Instructions:
1. Preheat your air fryer to 320°F (160°C) for 3 minutes. [Function used: Preheat]
2. In a mixing bowl, combine the mashed bananas, applesauce, honey, almond milk, and vanilla extract.
3. In another bowl, whisk together the whole wheat flour, baking powder, baking soda, cinnamon, and salt.
4. Gradually add the dry ingredients to the wet ingredients and mix until just combined.
5. Pour the batter into a greased air fryersafe baking pan.
6. Air fry for 2530 minutes, or until a toothpick inserted into the center comes out clean. [Function used: Air frying]
7. Allow the banana bread to cool before slicing and serving.

Nutritional Info (per serving): Calories: 150 | Fat: 1g | Carbs: 32g | Protein: 3g

Tip: For added sweetness, sprinkle a little cinnamon and honey on top before serving.

Cinnamon Sugar Doughnuts

Prep: 15 mins | Cook: 10 mins | Serves: 6 doughnuts

Ingredients:
- 1 cup all-purpose flour (US) / 120g plain flour (UK)
- 1/3 cup granulated sugar (US) / 70g caster sugar (UK)
- 1 teaspoon baking powder
- 1/4 teaspoon ground cinnamon
- 1/4 teaspoon salt
- 1/2 cup unsweetened almond milk (US) / 120ml unsweetened almond milk (UK)
- 1 egg
- 2 tablespoons unsalted butter, melted (US) / 30g unsalted butter, melted (UK)
- 1 teaspoon vanilla extract
- 1/4 cup granulated sugar + 1 teaspoon ground cinnamon, for coating (US) / 50g caster sugar + 1 teaspoon ground cinnamon, for coating (UK)
- Cooking spray

Instructions:
1. Preheat your air fryer to 350°F (180°C) for 3 minutes. [Function used: Preheat]
2. In a large bowl, whisk together the flour, sugar, baking powder, cinnamon, and salt.
3. In another bowl, whisk together the almond milk, egg, melted butter, and vanilla extract.
4. Gradually add the wet ingredients to the dry ingredients, stirring until just combined.
5. Lightly coat the doughnut molds of your air fryer with cooking spray.
6. Spoon the batter into the molds, filling each about 2/3 full.
7. Air fry for 8-10 minutes, or until the doughnuts are golden brown and cooked through. [Function used: Air frying]
8. In a shallow dish, mix together the granulated sugar and ground cinnamon for coating.
9. While the doughnuts are still warm, roll them in the cinnamon sugar mixture until coated.
10. Serve immediately and enjoy!

Nutritional Info (per serving): Calories: 200|Fat: 5g|Carbs:35g| Protein: 4g

Tip: Add a pinch of nutmeg or cardamom to the cinnamon sugar mixture for extra flavor.

Sweet Potato Hash

Prep: 10 mins | Cook: 20 mins | Serves: 4

Ingredients:
- 2 medium sweet potatoes, peeled and diced (US) / 2 medium sweet potatoes, peeled and diced (UK)
- 1 red bell pepper, diced
- 1 yellow onion, diced
- 2 cloves garlic, minced
- 2 tablespoons olive oil
- 1 teaspoon paprika
- 1/2 teaspoon dried thyme
- Salt and pepper, to taste
- Fresh parsley, chopped, for garnish

Instructions:
1. Preheat your air fryer to 375°F (190°C) for 3 minutes. [Function used: Preheat]
2. In a large mixing bowl, toss together the diced sweet potatoes, bell pepper, onion, minced garlic, olive oil, paprika, dried thyme, salt, and pepper until evenly coated.
3. Spread the mixture in a single layer in the air fryer basket.
4. Air fry for 1520 minutes, shaking the basket halfway through cooking, until the sweet potatoes are tender and golden brown. [Function used: Air frying]
5. Transfer the sweet potato hash to a serving dish, sprinkle with fresh parsley, and serve hot.

Nutritional Info (per serving): Calories: 180 | Fat: 7g | Carbs: 28g | Protein: 3g

Tip: Add diced cooked bacon or sausage for extra flavor and protein.

Blueberry Oatmeal Cups

Prep: 10 mins | Cook: 20 mins | Serves: 6 cups

Ingredients:
- 1 cup rolled oats (US) / 100g rolled oats (UK)
- 1/4 cup unsweetened applesauce (US) / 60ml unsweetened applesauce (UK)
- 1/4 cup milk (US) / 60ml milk (UK)
- 2 tablespoons honey (US) / 30ml honey (UK)
- 1/2 teaspoon vanilla extract
- 1/2 teaspoon ground cinnamon
- 1/4 teaspoon salt
- 1/2 cup blueberries (fresh or frozen)

Instructions:
1. Preheat your air fryer to 320°F (160°C) for 3 minutes. [Function used: Preheat]
2. In a mixing bowl, combine the rolled oats, applesauce, milk, honey, vanilla extract, cinnamon, and salt.
3. Gently fold in the blueberries.
4. Divide the mixture evenly among 6 silicone muffin cups.
5. Place the muffin cups in the air fryer basket.
6. Air fry for 1520 minutes, or until the oatmeal cups are set and lightly golden on top. [Function used: Air frying]
7. Allow the oatmeal cups to cool slightly before serving.

Nutritional Info (per serving): Calories: 120 | Fat: 2g | Carbs: 24g | Protein: 3g

Tip: Customize your oatmeal cups by adding chopped nuts or shredded coconut before baking.

VeggiePacked Breakfast Burrito

Prep: 15 mins | Cook: 10 mins | Serves: 2

Ingredients:
- 2 whole wheat tortillas (US) / 2 wholemeal tortillas (UK)
- 4 eggs
- 1/2 cup bell peppers, diced (US) / 60g bell peppers, diced (UK)
- 1/2 cup cherry tomatoes, halved (US) / 60g cherry tomatoes, halved (UK)
- 1/4 cup black beans, drained and rinsed (US) / 40g black beans, drained and rinsed (UK)
- 1/4 cup shredded cheddar cheese (US) / 30g shredded cheddar cheese (UK)
- Salt and pepper, to taste
- Cooking spray

Instructions:
1. Preheat your air fryer to 350°F (180°C) for 3 minutes. [Function used: Preheat]
2. In a bowl, whisk the eggs and season with salt and pepper.
3. Heat a skillet over medium heat and coat with cooking spray.
4. Pour the whisked eggs into the skillet and cook, stirring occasionally, until scrambled and cooked through.
5. Lay out the tortillas on a flat surface.
6. Divide the scrambled eggs, diced bell peppers, cherry tomatoes, black beans, and shredded cheddar cheese evenly between the tortillas.
7. Fold the sides of each tortilla over the filling, then roll up tightly to form burritos.
8. Place the burritos seamside down in the air fryer basket.
9. Air fry for 57 minutes, or until the tortillas are golden brown and crispy. [Function used: Air frying]
10. Serve hot and enjoy!

Nutritional Info (per serving): Calories: 350 | Fat: 16g | Carbs: 29g | Protein: 22g

Tip: Customize your breakfast burrito by adding avocado slices, salsa, or a dollop of Greek yogurt before serving.

Zucchini Bread

Prep: 15 mins | Cook: 35 mins | Serves: 8 slices

Ingredients:
- 2 cups grated zucchini (US) / 200g grated zucchini (UK)
- 1/2 cup unsweetened applesauce (US) / 120ml unsweetened applesauce (UK)
- 1/2 cup honey (US) / 120ml honey (UK)
- 2 eggs
- 1 teaspoon vanilla extract
- 1 1/2 cups whole wheat flour (US) / 180g wholemeal flour (UK)
- 1 teaspoon baking powder
- 1/2 teaspoon baking soda
- 1/2 teaspoon ground cinnamon
- 1/4 teaspoon salt

Instructions:
1. Preheat your air fryer to 320°F (160°C) for 3 minutes. [Function used: Preheat]
2. In a large bowl, combine the grated zucchini, applesauce, honey, eggs, and vanilla extract.
3. In another bowl, whisk together the whole wheat flour, baking powder, baking soda, cinnamon, and salt.
4. Gradually add the dry ingredients to the wet ingredients, stirring until just combined.
5. Pour the batter into a greased air fryersafe loaf pan.
6. Air fry for 3035 minutes, or until a toothpick inserted into the center comes out clean. [Function used: Air frying]
7. Allow the zucchini bread to cool in the pan for 10 minutes before transferring to a wire rack to cool completely.

Nutritional Info (per serving): Calories: 200 | Fat: 2g | Carbs: 40g | Protein: 5g

Tip: Add chopped nuts or raisins to the batter for extra texture and flavor.

Protein Packed Granola

Prep: 10 mins | Cook: 20 mins | Serves: 6 servings

Ingredients:
- 2 cups rolled oats (US) / 200g rolled oats (UK)
- 1/2 cup mixed nuts and seeds (such as almonds, walnuts, pumpkin seeds, sunflower seeds)
- 1/4 cup unsweetened shredded coconut
- 2 tablespoons coconut oil, melted
- 2 tablespoons honey or maple syrup
- 1 teaspoon vanilla extract
- Pinch of salt
- 1/2 cup dried fruit (such as raisins, cranberries), optional

Instructions:
1. Preheat your air fryer to 300°F (150°C) for 3 minutes. [Function used: Preheat]
2. In a large mixing bowl, combine the rolled oats, mixed nuts and seeds, shredded coconut, melted coconut oil, honey or maple syrup, vanilla extract, and a pinch of salt. Stir well to combine and ensure the oats are evenly coated.
3. Spread the granola mixture evenly on the air fryer basket.
4. Air fry for 1520 minutes, stirring every 5 minutes to ensure even cooking, until the granola is golden brown and crispy. [Function used: Air frying]
5. Allow the granola to cool completely before adding dried fruit, if using.
6. Store the granola in an airtight container at room temperature for up to two weeks.

Nutritional Info (per serving): Calories: 250 | Fat: 15g | Carbs: 25g | Protein: 6g

Tip: Customize your granola by adding your favorite nuts, seeds, and dried fruits for variety.

Egg Muffins with Vegetables

Prep: 10 mins | Cook: 15 mins | Serves: 6 muffins

Ingredients:
- 6 eggs
- 1/4 cup milk (US) / 60ml milk (UK)
- 1/2 cup mixed vegetables, diced (such as bell peppers, onions, spinach)
- 1/4 cup shredded cheddar cheese
- Salt and pepper, to taste
- Cooking spray or olive oil, for greasing the muffin tin

Instructions:
1. Preheat your air fryer to 350°F (180°C) for 3 minutes. [Function used: Preheat]
2. In a mixing bowl, whisk together the eggs and milk until well combined.
3. Stir in the diced mixed vegetables and shredded cheddar cheese. Season with salt and pepper.
4. Grease a muffin tin with cooking spray or olive oil.
5. Pour the egg mixture evenly into the muffin tin, filling each cup about 3/4 full.
6. Place the muffin tin in the air fryer basket.
7. Air fry for 1215 minutes, or until the egg muffins are set and lightly golden on top.
8. Allow the egg muffins to cool slightly before removing them from the muffin tin.
9. Serve warm or at room temperature.

Nutritional Info (per serving): Calories: 120 | Fat: 8g | Carbs: 3g | Protein: 9g

Tip: Feel free to customize the egg muffins with your favorite vegetables and cheese for added flavor.

Greek Yogurt Parfait with Berries

Prep: 5 mins | Cook: 0 mins | Serves: 2

Ingredients:
- 1 cup Greek yogurt (US) / 250g Greek yogurt (UK)
- 1/2 cup mixed berries (such as strawberries, blueberries, and raspberries)
- 2 tablespoons granola (choose a lowsugar option)
- 1 tablespoon honey (optional)

Instructions:
1. In two serving glasses or bowls, layer the Greek yogurt, mixed berries, and granola.
2. Drizzle with honey, if desired.
3. Serve immediately and enjoy!

Nutritional Info (per serving): Calories: 200 | Fat: 3g | Carbs: 25g | Protein: 15g

Tip: Use unsweetened Greek yogurt and add a touch of sweetness with honey for a healthier option.

Savory Oatmeal with Mushrooms and Spinach

Prep: 5 mins | Cook: 10 mins | Serves: 2

Ingredients:
- 1 cup rolled oats (US) / 100g rolled oats (UK)
- 2 cups water or vegetable broth
- 1 cup mushrooms, sliced and 1 clove garlic, minced
- 1 cup fresh spinach leaves
- Salt and pepper, to taste
- Optional toppings: shredded cheese, chopped green onions

Instructions:
1. In a saucepan, bring the water or vegetable broth to a boil.
2. Stir in the rolled oats and reduce the heat to low. Cook, stirring occasionally, for about 5 minutes or until the oats are cooked and creamy.
3. Meanwhile, heat a skillet over medium heat and add the sliced mushrooms. Cook for 34 minutes until they begin to soften.
4. Add the minced garlic and spinach leaves to the skillet. Cook for an additional 23 minutes until the spinach wilts.
5. Season the mushroomspinach mixture with salt and pepper to taste.
6. Divide the cooked oatmeal between two bowls and top with the mushroomspinach mixture.
7. Garnish with optional toppings such as shredded cheese or chopped green onions.
8. Serve hot and enjoy!

Nutritional Info (per serving): Calories: 250 | Fat: 3g | Carbs: 45g | Protein: 10g

Tip: Experiment with different vegetables and seasonings to customize your savory oatmeal.

Whole Wheat Pancakes

Prep: 10 mins | Cook: 10 mins | Serves: 4

Ingredients:
- 1 cup whole wheat flour (US) / 120g wholemeal flour (UK)
- 1 tablespoon baking powder
- 1 tablespoon granulated sugar (or your preferred sugar substitute)
- 1/4 teaspoon salt
- 1 cup milk (US) / 240ml milk (UK)
- 1 egg
- 2 tablespoons unsalted butter, melted (US) / 30g unsalted butter, melted (UK)
- Cooking spray or additional butter, for greasing the pan

Instructions:
1. In a large mixing bowl, whisk together the whole wheat flour, baking powder, sugar, and salt.

2. In another bowl, whisk together the milk, egg, and melted butter.
3. Pour the wet ingredients into the dry ingredients and stir until just combined. Do not overmix; some lumps are okay.
4. Heat a nonstick skillet or griddle over medium heat and lightly grease with cooking spray or butter.
5. Pour about 1/4 cup of batter onto the skillet for each pancake.
6. Cook for 23 minutes on one side, until bubbles form on the surface.
7. Flip the pancakes and cook for an additional 12 minutes until golden brown and cooked through.
8. Repeat with the remaining batter, greasing the skillet as needed.
9. Serve the pancakes warm with your favorite toppings such as fresh fruit, Greek yogurt, or a drizzle of maple syrup.

Nutritional Info (per serving): Calories: 200 | Fat: 6g | Carbs: 30g | Protein: 7g
Tip: For extra fiber and texture, add rolled oats or ground flaxseed to the batter.

Overnight Chia Pudding

Prep: 5 mins | Cook: 0 mins | Serves: 2
Ingredients:
- 1/4 cup chia seeds (US) / 40g chia seeds (UK)
- 1 cup unsweetened almond milk (US) / 240ml unsweetened almond milk (UK)
- 1 tablespoon honey or maple syrup (optional)
- 1/2 teaspoon vanilla extract
- Toppings: fresh fruit, nuts, shredded coconut

Instructions:
1. In a mixing bowl or jar, combine the chia seeds, almond milk, honey or maple syrup (if using), and vanilla extract.
2. Stir well to combine.
3. Cover and refrigerate the mixture for at least 4 hours or overnight, allowing the chia seeds to absorb the liquid and thicken.
4. Before serving, give the chia pudding a good stir to evenly distribute the seeds.
5. Divide the pudding between two serving bowls or glasses.
6. Top with your favorite toppings such as fresh fruit, nuts, or shredded coconut.
7. Serve chilled and enjoy!

Nutritional Info (per serving): Calories: 150 | Fat: 8g | Carbs: 15g | Protein: 5g
Tip: Experiment with different flavors by adding cocoa powder, cinnamon, or mashed fruit to the pudding mixture before refrigerating.

Breakfast Cauliflower Rice Bowls

Prep: 10 mins | Cook: 15 mins | Serves: 4

Ingredients:
- 1 medium cauliflower head, grated (US) / 1 medium cauliflower head, grated (UK)
- 1 tablespoon olive oil
- 1/2 teaspoon garlic powder
- 1/2 teaspoon onion powder
- Salt and pepper, to taste
- 4 eggs
- 1 avocado, sliced
- Optional toppings: diced tomatoes, sliced green onions, salsa

Instructions:
1. Preheat your air fryer to 375°F (190°C) for 3 minutes. [Function used: Preheat]
2. In a mixing bowl, toss together the grated cauliflower, olive oil, garlic powder, onion powder, salt, and pepper until evenly coated.
3. Spread the cauliflower mixture in a single layer in the air fryer basket.
4. Air fry for 12-15 minutes, shaking the basket halfway through cooking, until the cauliflower is tender and golden brown. [Function used: Air frying]
5. While the cauliflower rice is cooking, prepare the eggs to your liking (scrambled, fried, or poached).
6. Divide the cooked cauliflower rice between four bowls.
7. Top each bowl with a cooked egg, sliced avocado, and any additional toppings of your choice.
8. Serve hot and enjoy!

Nutritional Info (per serving): Calories: 200 | Fat: 12g | Carbs: 10g | Protein: 10g

Tip: For extra protein, add cooked chicken or tofu to the cauliflower rice bowls. You can also customize the toppings to suit your taste preferences.

CHAPTER 3: APPETIZERS AND SNACKS

Crispy Chickpeas

Prep: 5 mins | Cook: 20 mins | Serves: 4

Ingredients:
- 1 can (15 oz) chickpeas, drained and rinsed (US) / 1 can (400g) chickpeas, drained and rinsed (UK)
- 1 tablespoon olive oil
- 1 teaspoon ground cumin
- 1/2 teaspoon paprika
- 1/2 teaspoon garlic powder
- Salt and pepper, to taste

Instructions:
1. Preheat your air fryer to 390°F (200°C) for 3 minutes. [Function used: Preheat]
2. Pat the chickpeas dry with a paper towel to remove excess moisture.
3. In a bowl, toss the chickpeas with olive oil, ground cumin, paprika, garlic powder, salt, and pepper until evenly coated.
4. Spread the seasoned chickpeas in a single layer in the air fryer basket.
5. Air fry for 1520 minutes, shaking the basket halfway through cooking, until the chickpeas are crispy and golden brown. [Function used: Air frying]
6. Remove from the air fryer, let cool slightly, and serve as a crunchy snack or salad topper.

Nutritional Info (per serving): Calories: 150 | Fat: 5g | Carbs: 20g | Protein: 6g

Tip: Customize the seasoning with your favorite spices like chili powder or smoked paprika for added flavor.

Zucchini Fries

Prep: 10 mins | Cook: 12 mins | Serves: 4

Ingredients:
- 2 medium zucchinis, cut into fries (US) / 2 medium courgettes, cut into fries (UK)
- 1/2 cup breadcrumbs (use whole wheat for a healthier option)
- 1/4 cup grated Parmesan cheese
- 1 teaspoon Italian seasoning
- 1/2 teaspoon garlic powder
- 1/4 teaspoon salt
- 1/4 teaspoon black pepper
- 2 eggs, beaten

Instructions:
1. Preheat your air fryer to 400°F (200°C) for 3 minutes. [Function used: Preheat]
2. In a shallow dish, combine the breadcrumbs, Parmesan cheese, Italian seasoning, garlic powder, salt, and black pepper.
3. Dip each zucchini fry into the beaten eggs, then coat evenly with the breadcrumb mixture.
4. Place the coated zucchini fries in a single layer in the air fryer basket, making sure they are not touching.
5. Air fry for 1012 minutes, flipping halfway through cooking, until the zucchini fries are golden and crispy. [Function used: Air frying]
6. Serve hot with your favorite dipping sauce, such as marinara or Greek yogurt mixed with herbs.

Nutritional Info (per serving): Calories: 120 | Fat: 4g | Carbs: 15g | Protein: 7g

Tip: For extra crispiness, spray the zucchini fries lightly with cooking spray before air frying.

Garlic Parmesan Kale Chips

Prep: 10 mins | Cook: 10 mins | Serves: 4

Ingredients:
- 1 bunch kale, stems removed and leaves torn into bitesized pieces (US & UK)
- 1 tablespoon olive oil
- 1/4 cup grated Parmesan cheese
- 2 cloves garlic, minced
- Salt, to taste

Instructions:
1. Preheat your air fryer to 375°F (190°C) for 3 minutes. [Function used: Preheat]
2. In a large bowl, massage the torn kale leaves with olive oil until evenly coated.
3. Sprinkle minced garlic and grated Parmesan cheese over the kale leaves, and toss to combine.
4. Spread the seasoned kale leaves in a single layer in the air fryer basket.
5. Air fry for 810 minutes, shaking the basket halfway through cooking, until the kale chips are crispy and lightly browned. [Function used: Air frying]
6. Remove from the air fryer, sprinkle with salt to taste, and let cool slightly before serving.

Nutritional Info (per serving): Calories: 70 | Fat: 4g | Carbs: 6g | Protein: 3g

Tip: Keep an eye on the kale chips during cooking to prevent burning, as cooking times may vary depending on the size and thickness of the leaves.

Avocado Fries

Prep: 15 mins | Cook: 8 mins | Serves: 2

Ingredients:
- 1 large ripe avocado, sliced into fries (US & UK)
- 1/4 cup flour (US & UK)
- 1 egg, beaten
- 3/4 cup breadcrumbs (use whole wheat for a healthier option) (US & UK)
- 1/2 teaspoon garlic powder
- 1/2 teaspoon paprika
- Salt and pepper, to taste

Instructions:
1. Preheat your air fryer to 375°F (190°C) for 3 minutes. [Function used: Preheat]
2. Set up a breading station with three shallow dishes: one with flour, one with beaten egg, and one with breadcrumbs mixed with garlic powder, paprika, salt, and pepper.
3. Dredge each avocado slice in the flour, shaking off any excess.
4. Dip the floured avocado slice into the beaten egg, allowing any excess to drip off.
5. Coat the avocado slice in the seasoned breadcrumb mixture, pressing gently to adhere.
6. Place the breaded avocado slices in a single layer in the air fryer basket, without overcrowding.
7. Air fry for 68 minutes, turning halfway through cooking, until the avocado fries are golden and crispy. [Function used: Air frying]
8. Serve immediately with your favorite dipping sauce, such as ranch dressing or salsa.

Nutritional Info (per serving): Calories: 250 | Fat: 15g | Carbs: 25g | Protein: 7g

Tip: For an extra crunchy coating, you can double coat the avocado slices by repeating the egg and breadcrumb steps.

Baked Sweet Potato Chips

Prep: 15 mins | Cook: 12 mins | Serves: 4

Ingredients:
- 2 medium sweet potatoes, scrubbed and thinly sliced (US) / 2 medium sweet potatoes, scrubbed and thinly sliced (UK)
- 1 tablespoon olive oil
- 1 teaspoon paprika
- 1/2 teaspoon garlic powder
- 1/2 teaspoon onion powder
- Salt and pepper, to taste

Instructions:
1. Preheat your air fryer to 380°F (190°C) for 3 minutes. [Function used: Preheat]
2. In a large bowl, toss the sweet potato slices with olive oil, paprika, garlic powder, onion powder, salt, and pepper until evenly coated.
3. Spread the seasoned sweet potato slices in a single layer in the air fryer basket.
4. Air fry for 1012 minutes, flipping halfway through cooking, until the sweet potato chips are crispy and lightly browned. [Function used: Air frying]
5. Remove from the air fryer and let cool slightly before serving.
6. Serve as a crunchy snack or a healthier alternative to regular potato chips.

Nutritional Info (per serving): Calories: 120 | Fat: 3g | Carbs: 22g | Protein: 2g

Tip: Keep an eye on the sweet potato chips during cooking as they can burn easily due to their natural sugars.

Cauliflower Buffalo Wings

Prep: 15 mins | Cook: 20 mins | Serves: 4

Ingredients:
- 1 head cauliflower, cut into florets (US & UK)
- 1/2 cup all-purpose flour (US & UK)
- 1/2 cup water
- 1 teaspoon garlic powder
- 1/2 teaspoon onion powder
- Salt and pepper, to taste
- 1/2 cup buffalo sauce
- Cooking spray

Instructions:
1. Preheat your air fryer to 375°F (190°C) for 3 minutes. [Function used: Preheat]
2. In a bowl, whisk together the all-purpose flour, water, garlic powder, onion powder, salt, and pepper until smooth to create the batter.
3. Dip each cauliflower floret into the batter, shaking off any excess.
4. Place the battered cauliflower florets in a single layer in the air fryer basket, without overcrowding.
5. Air fry for 10 minutes, flipping halfway through cooking, until the cauliflower is golden and crispy. [Function used: Air frying]
6. Remove the cauliflower from the air fryer and toss with buffalo sauce until evenly coated.
7. Return the cauliflower to the air fryer basket and air fry for an additional 57 minutes until the buffalo sauce is caramelized and sticky.
8. Serve hot with ranch dressing or your favorite dipping sauce.

Nutritional Info (per serving): Calories: 100 | Fat: 1g | Carbs: 20g | Protein: 4g

Tip: Adjust the amount of buffalo sauce according to your spice preference for milder or spicier wings.

Cucumber Bites with Tzatziki

Prep: 15 mins | Cook: 0 mins | Serves: 4

Ingredients:
- 2 large cucumbers, sliced into rounds (US & UK)
- 1 cup Greek yogurt (US & UK)
- 1/2 cucumber, finely diced (US & UK)
- 1 clove garlic, minced
- 1 tablespoon fresh dill, chopped
- 1 tablespoon lemon juice
- Salt and pepper, to taste
- Fresh dill or mint leaves, for garnish

Instructions:
1. In a bowl, combine Greek yogurt, diced cucumber, minced garlic, chopped dill, lemon juice, salt, and pepper to make the tzatziki sauce.
2. Stir until well combined, then refrigerate for at least 10 minutes to allow the flavors to meld.
3. Arrange the cucumber rounds on a serving platter.
4. Spoon a dollop of tzatziki sauce onto each cucumber round.
5. Garnish with fresh dill or mint leaves.
6. Serve immediately as a refreshing appetizer or snack.

Nutritional Info (per serving): Calories: 50 | Fat: 1g | Carbs: 6g | Protein: 5g

Tip: You can sprinkle some paprika or sumac on top for extra flavor and visual appeal.

Roasted Edamame

Prep: 5 mins | Cook: 15 mins | Serves: 4

Ingredients:
- 2 cups frozen shelled edamame (US & UK)
- 1 tablespoon olive oil
- 1 teaspoon garlic powder
- 1/2 teaspoon smoked paprika
- 1/4 teaspoon cayenne pepper (optional)
- Salt, to taste

Instructions:
1. Preheat your air fryer to 375°F (190°C) for 3 minutes. [Function used: Preheat]
2. In a bowl, toss frozen edamame with olive oil, garlic powder, smoked paprika, cayenne pepper (if using), and salt until well coated.
3. Spread the seasoned edamame in a single layer in the air fryer basket.
4. Air fry for 1215 minutes, shaking the basket halfway through cooking, until the edamame is crispy and lightly browned. [Function used: Air frying]
5. Remove from the air fryer and let cool slightly before serving.
6. Enjoy as a nutritious and crunchy snack.

Nutritional Info (per serving): Calories: 120 | Fat: 5g | Carbs: 9g | Protein: 9g

Tip: Experiment with different seasonings such as chili powder or soy sauce for variation.

Baked Avocado Boats

Prep: 10 mins | Cook: 12 mins | Serves: 2

Ingredients:
- 1 ripe avocado, halved and pitted (US & UK)
- 2 eggs
- Salt and pepper, to taste
- Optional toppings: diced tomatoes, chopped cilantro, shredded cheese

Instructions:
1. Preheat your air fryer to 375°F (190°C) for 3 minutes. [Function used: Preheat]
2. Scoop out a small portion of the avocado flesh from each half to create a well for the egg.
3. Crack one egg into each avocado half, making sure the yolk stays intact.
4. Season with salt and pepper to taste.
5. Place the avocado halves in the air fryer basket, balancing them to prevent tipping over.
6. Air fry for 1012 minutes, or until the egg whites are set and the yolks reach your desired consistency. [Function used: Air frying]
7. Remove from the air fryer and let cool slightly.
8. Garnish with optional toppings such as diced tomatoes, chopped cilantro, or shredded cheese.
9. Serve hot and enjoy these delicious and nutritious baked avocado boats!

Nutritional Info (per serving): Calories: 220 | Fat: 18g | Carbs: 8g | Protein: 9g

Tip: For added flavor, sprinkle some crumbled bacon or hot sauce on top before serving.

Roasted Beet Hummus

Prep: 10 mins | Cook: 0 mins | Serves: 8

Ingredients:
- 1 can (15 oz) chickpeas, drained and rinsed (US & UK)
- 1 medium beet, roasted and peeled (US & UK)
- 2 tablespoons tahini
- 2 tablespoons lemon juice
- 2 cloves garlic, minced
- 2 tablespoons olive oil
- Salt and pepper, to taste
- Water, as needed
- Optional garnishes: olive oil, sesame seeds, chopped fresh herbs

Instructions:
1. In a food processor, combine chickpeas, roasted beet, tahini, lemon juice, minced garlic, olive oil, salt, and pepper.
2. Blend until smooth, scraping down the sides of the bowl as needed.
3. If the hummus is too thick, add water, 1 tablespoon at a time, until desired consistency is reached.
4. Taste and adjust seasoning if necessary.
5. Transfer the beet hummus to a serving bowl and drizzle with olive oil.
6. Garnish with sesame seeds and chopped fresh herbs, if desired.
7. Serve with pita bread, vegetable sticks, or crackers for a colorful and flavorful snack or appetizer.

Nutritional Info (per serving): Calories: 120 | Fat: 6g | Carbs: 14g | Protein: 4g

Tip: You can roast the beet in the air fryer before making the hummus. Simply wrap the beet in foil and air fry at 400°F (200°C) for 3040 minutes, or until tender. Let it cool, then peel and use in the recipe.

AirFried Deviled Eggs

Prep: 15 mins | Cook: 10 mins | Serves: 6

Ingredients:
- 6 large eggs
- 2 tablespoons mayonnaise (US & UK)
- 1 teaspoon Dijon mustard
- 1 teaspoon white vinegar
- 1/4 teaspoon salt
- 1/4 teaspoon black pepper
- Paprika, for garnish
- Chopped fresh chives, for garnish

Instructions:
1. Place the eggs in a single layer in the air fryer basket.
2. Air fry at 270°F (132°C) for 15 minutes. [Function used: Air frying]
3. Once cooked, transfer the eggs to an ice bath and let them cool completely.
4. Once cooled, peel the eggs and cut them in half lengthwise. Remove the yolks and place them in a bowl.
5. Mash the egg yolks with mayonnaise, Dijon mustard, white vinegar, salt, and black pepper until smooth.
6. Spoon or pipe the yolk mixture into the egg white halves.
7. Sprinkle with paprika and chopped fresh chives for garnish.
8. Serve chilled and enjoy these flavorful airfried deviled eggs as a delightful appetizer.

Nutritional Info (per serving): Calories: 80 | Fat: 6g | Carbs: 1g | Protein: 6g

Tip: For an extra kick, add a pinch of cayenne pepper or hot sauce to the yolk mixture.

Crispy Tofu Bites

Prep: 15 mins | Cook: 15 mins | Serves: 4

Ingredients:
- 1 block (14 oz) firm tofu, pressed and cubed (US & UK)
- 2 tablespoons cornstarch (US & UK)
- 1 tablespoon soy sauce
- 1 tablespoon rice vinegar
- 1 tablespoon maple syrup
- 1 teaspoon sesame oil
- 1/2 teaspoon garlic powder
- 1/2 teaspoon onion powder
- Cooking spray

Instructions:
1. Preheat your air fryer to 400°F (200°C) for 3 minutes. [Function used: Preheat]
2. In a bowl, whisk together soy sauce, rice vinegar, maple syrup, sesame oil, garlic powder, and onion powder to make the marinade.
3. Toss the cubed tofu in the marinade until well coated.
4. Sprinkle cornstarch over the tofu cubes and toss until evenly coated.
5. Lightly spray the air fryer basket with cooking spray.
6. Arrange the tofu cubes in a single layer in the air fryer basket.
7. Air fry for 1215 minutes, shaking the basket halfway through cooking, until the tofu is crispy and golden brown. [Function used: Air frying]
8. Serve hot with your favorite dipping sauce or as a proteinpacked snack.

Nutritional Info (per serving): Calories: 120 | Fat: 4g | Carbs: 10g | Protein: 10g

Tip: Serve with sweet chili sauce or teriyaki sauce for extra flavor.

AirFried Falafel

Prep: 15 mins | Cook: 12 mins | Serves: 4

Ingredients:
- 1 can (15 oz) chickpeas, drained and rinsed (US & UK)
- 1/4 cup chopped fresh parsley
- 1/4 cup chopped fresh cilantro
- 2 cloves garlic, minced
- 1 teaspoon ground cumin
- 1 teaspoon ground coriander
- 1/2 teaspoon baking powder
- Salt and pepper, to taste
- Cooking spray

Instructions:
1. In a food processor, combine chickpeas, chopped parsley, chopped cilantro, minced garlic, ground cumin, ground coriander, baking powder, salt, and pepper.
2. Pulse until the mixture is well combined but still slightly chunky.
3. Shape the mixture into small balls or patties, about 1 inch in diameter.
4. Lightly spray the air fryer basket with cooking spray.
5. Arrange the falafel balls or patties in a single layer in the air fryer basket.
6. Air fry at 370°F (187°C) for 1012 minutes, flipping halfway through cooking, until the falafel is crispy and golden brown. [Function used: Air frying]
7. Serve hot with tahini sauce, hummus, or yogurt sauce.

Nutritional Info (per serving): Calories: 120 | Fat: 3g | Carbs: 18g | Protein: 6g

Tip: For a smoother texture, you can blend the mixture in the food processor until smooth before shaping into balls or patties.

Caprese Skewers

Prep: 10 mins | Cook: 0 mins | Serves: 4

Ingredients:
- 1 pint cherry tomatoes (US & UK)
- 8 oz fresh mozzarella balls (US & UK)
- Balsamic glaze, for drizzling and Fresh basil leaves
- Wooden skewers

Instructions:
1. Thread one cherry tomato, one mozzarella ball, and one basil leaf onto each wooden skewer, repeating until all ingredients are used.
2. Arrange the skewers on a serving platter.
3. Drizzle with balsamic glaze.
4. Serve immediately as a light and refreshing appetizer or snack.

Nutritional Info (per serving): Calories: 100 | Fat: 6g | Carbs: 4g | Protein: 8g

Tip: You can sprinkle the skewers with a pinch of salt and pepper for extra flavor.

Sweet and Spicy Nuts

Prep: 5 mins | Cook: 10 mins | Serves: 6

Ingredients:
- 2 cups mixed nuts (such as almonds, cashews, peanuts) (US & UK)
- 2 tablespoons maple syrup
- 1 tablespoon olive oil and 1 teaspoon chili powder
- 1/2 teaspoon ground cinnamon
- 1/4 teaspoon cayenne pepper (optional)
- Salt, to taste

Instructions:
1. Preheat your air fryer to 350°F (175°C) for 3 minutes. [Function used: Preheat]
2. In a bowl, toss mixed nuts with maple syrup, olive oil, chili powder, ground cinnamon, cayenne pepper (if using), and salt until evenly coated.
3. Spread the seasoned nuts in a single layer in the air fryer basket.
4. Air fry for 810 minutes, shaking the basket halfway through cooking, until the nuts are toasted and fragrant. [Function used: Air frying]
5. Remove from the air fryer and let cool slightly before serving.
6. Enjoy as a sweet and spicy snack or appetizer.

Nutritional Info (per serving): Calories: 200 | Fat: 16g | Carbs: 10g | Protein: 6g

Tip: Store any leftovers in an airtight container at room temperature for up to one week.

CHAPTER 4: SOUPS AND SALADS

Creamy Broccoli Soup

Prep: 10 mins | Cook: 20 mins | Serves: 4

Ingredients:
- 4 cups broccoli florets (US & UK)
- 1 onion, diced (US & UK)
- 2 cloves garlic, minced (US & UK)
- 4 cups lowsodium vegetable broth (US & UK)
- 1/2 cup unsweetened almond milk (US & UK)
- Salt and pepper, to taste
- Optional toppings: grated cheese, crumbled bacon

Instructions:
1. Preheat your air fryer to 375°F (190°C) for 3 minutes. [Function used: Preheat]
2. Place broccoli florets, diced onion, and minced garlic in the air fryer basket.
3. Air fry for 1012 minutes until vegetables are tender. [Function used: Air frying]
4. Transfer the airfried vegetables to a blender.
5. Add vegetable broth and almond milk to the blender. Blend until smooth.
6. Pour the blended mixture into a pot and bring to a simmer.
7. Season with salt and pepper to taste.
8. Serve hot with optional toppings like grated cheese or crumbled bacon.

Nutritional Info (per serving): Calories: 80 | Fat: 2g | Carbs: 12g | Protein: 4g

Tip: For extra creaminess, blend in a handful of soaked cashews with the vegetables.

Lentil and Vegetable Soup

Prep: 15 mins | Cook: 25 mins | Serves: 6

Ingredients:
- ✓ 1 cup dried lentils, rinsed (US & UK)
- ✓ 1 onion, diced (US & UK)
- ✓ 2 carrots, diced (US & UK)
- ✓ 2 celery stalks, diced (US & UK)
- ✓ 2 cloves garlic, minced (US & UK)
- ✓ 6 cups lowsodium vegetable broth (US & UK)
- ✓ 1 teaspoon dried thyme
- ✓ 1 teaspoon dried oregano
- ✓ Salt and pepper, to taste

Instructions:
1. Preheat your air fryer to 375°F (190°C) for 3 minutes. [Function used: Preheat]
2. Place diced onion, carrots, celery, and minced garlic in the air fryer basket.
3. Air fry for 810 minutes until vegetables are tender. [Function used: Air frying]
4. In a pot, combine airfried vegetables, rinsed lentils, vegetable broth, dried thyme, and dried oregano.
5. Bring to a boil, then reduce heat and simmer for 1520 minutes until lentils are cooked.
6. Season with salt and pepper to taste.
7. Serve hot as a nutritious and filling soup option.

Nutritional Info (per serving): Calories: 180 | Fat: 1g | Carbs: 32g | Protein: 11g

Tip: Add a splash of balsamic vinegar for extra flavor before serving.

Tomato Basil Soup

Prep: 10 mins | Cook: 20 mins | Serves: 4

Ingredients:
- 1 can (14 oz) diced tomatoes (US & UK)
- 1 onion, diced (US & UK)
- 2 cloves garlic, minced (US & UK)
- 4 cups lowsodium vegetable broth (US & UK)
- 1/4 cup fresh basil leaves, chopped (US & UK)
- 1 teaspoon dried oregano
- Salt and pepper, to taste
- Optional garnish: fresh basil leaves, grated Parmesan cheese

Instructions:
1. Preheat your air fryer to 375°F (190°C) for 3 minutes. [Function used: Preheat]
2. Place diced onion and minced garlic in the air fryer basket.
3. Air fry for 810 minutes until onion is translucent and fragrant. [Function used: Air frying]
4. Add diced tomatoes (with juices), lowsodium vegetable broth, chopped basil leaves, and dried oregano to the air fryer basket with the onion and garlic.
5. Air fry for another 5 minutes until heated through.
6. Transfer the mixture to a blender and blend until smooth.
7. Pour the blended soup into a pot and bring to a simmer.
8. Season with salt and pepper to taste.
9. Serve hot with optional garnish like fresh basil leaves or grated Parmesan cheese.

Nutritional Info (per serving): Calories: 70 | Fat: 0.5g | Carbs: 14g | Protein: 3g

Tip: For a richer flavor, add a splash of balsamic vinegar or a dollop of Greek yogurt before serving.

Butternut Squash Soup

Prep: 15 mins | Cook: 25 mins | Serves: 6

Ingredients:
- 1 medium butternut squash, peeled, seeded, and cubed (US & UK)
- 1 onion, diced (US & UK)
- 2 carrots, diced (US & UK)
- 2 cloves garlic, minced (US & UK)
- 4 cups lowsodium vegetable broth (US & UK)
- 1 teaspoon dried thyme
- 1/2 teaspoon ground nutmeg
- Salt and pepper, to taste
- Optional garnish: Greek yogurt, pumpkin seeds

Instructions:
1. Preheat your air fryer to 375°F (190°C) for 3 minutes. [Function used: Preheat]
2. Place cubed butternut squash, diced onion, diced carrots, and minced garlic in the air fryer basket.
3. Air fry for 1215 minutes until vegetables are tender. [Function used: Air frying]
4. In a pot, combine airfried vegetables, lowsodium vegetable broth, dried thyme, and ground nutmeg.
5. Bring to a boil, then reduce heat and simmer for 1012 minutes.
6. Use an immersion blender to blend the soup until smooth.
7. Season with salt and pepper to taste.
8. Serve hot with optional garnish like a dollop of Greek yogurt or sprinkled pumpkin seeds.

Nutritional Info (per serving): Calories: 100 | Fat: 0.5g | Carbs: 24g | Protein: 2g

Tip: For added sweetness, roast the cubed butternut squash in the air fryer before making the soup.

Chicken and Veggie Soup

Prep: 15 mins | Cook: 25 mins | Serves: 4

Ingredients:
- ✓ 2 boneless, skinless chicken breasts, cubed (US & UK)
- ✓ 2 carrots, diced (US & UK)
- ✓ 2 celery stalks, diced (US & UK)
- ✓ 1 onion, diced (US & UK)
- ✓ 2 cloves garlic, minced (US & UK)
- ✓ 6 cups lowsodium chicken broth (US & UK)
- ✓ 1 teaspoon dried thyme
- ✓ Salt and pepper, to taste
- ✓ Fresh parsley, for garnish

Instructions:
1. Preheat your air fryer to 375°F (190°C) for 3 minutes. [Function used: Preheat]
2. Place cubed chicken breasts, diced carrots, diced celery, diced onion, and minced garlic in the air fryer basket.
3. Air fry for 1012 minutes until chicken is cooked through and vegetables are tender. [Function used: Air frying]
4. In a pot, combine airfried chicken and vegetables with lowsodium chicken broth and dried thyme.
5. Bring to a boil, then reduce heat and simmer for 1015 minutes.
6. Season with salt and pepper to taste.
7. Serve hot, garnished with fresh parsley.

Nutritional Info (per serving): Calories: 150 | Fat: 3g | Carbs: 6g | Protein: 25g

Tip: Add a squeeze of lemon juice for a refreshing twist before serving.

Spinach Salad with Warm Bacon Dressing

Prep: 10 mins | Cook: 10 mins | Serves: 4

Ingredients:
- 6 cups fresh spinach leaves (US & UK)
- 4 slices bacon, chopped (US & UK)
- 1/4 cup red onion, thinly sliced (US & UK)
- 1/4 cup cherry tomatoes, halved (US & UK)
- 1/4 cup sliced almonds, toasted (US & UK)
- 2 tablespoons apple cider vinegar
- 1 tablespoon olive oil
- 1 teaspoon Dijon mustard
- Salt and pepper, to taste

Instructions:
1. Place chopped bacon in the air fryer basket.
2. Air fry at 370°F (187°C) for 810 minutes until bacon is crispy. [Function used: Air frying]
3. Remove bacon from the air fryer and transfer to a plate lined with paper towels to drain excess grease.
4. In a small bowl, whisk together apple cider vinegar, olive oil, Dijon mustard, salt, and pepper to make the dressing.
5. In a large bowl, add fresh spinach leaves, thinly sliced red onion, halved cherry tomatoes, and toasted sliced almonds.
6. Pour the warm bacon dressing over the salad ingredients.
7. Toss the salad gently until the dressing is evenly distributed.
8. Serve immediately as a delicious and nutritious salad option.

Nutritional Info (per serving): Calories: 160 | Fat: 12g | Carbs: 6g | Protein: 8g

Tip: You can substitute turkey bacon for regular bacon to reduce the fat content.

Greek Salad

Prep: 15 mins | Cook: 0 mins | Serves: 4

Ingredients:
- 2 cups cherry tomatoes, halved (US & UK)
- 1 cucumber, diced (US & UK)
- 1 red bell pepper, diced (US & UK)
- 1/2 red onion, thinly sliced (US & UK)
- 1/2 cup Kalamata olives (US & UK)
- 4 oz feta cheese, crumbled (US & UK)
- 2 tablespoons extra virgin olive oil (US & UK)
- 1 tablespoon red wine vinegar (US & UK)
- 1 teaspoon dried oregano (US & UK)
- Salt and pepper, to taste
- Fresh parsley, for garnish

Instructions:
1. In a large bowl, combine cherry tomatoes, diced cucumber, diced red bell pepper, thinly sliced red onion, and Kalamata olives.
2. In a small bowl, whisk together extra virgin olive oil, red wine vinegar, dried oregano, salt, and pepper to make the dressing.
3. Pour the dressing over the salad ingredients and toss until well coated.
4. Sprinkle crumbled feta cheese over the salad.
5. Garnish with fresh parsley.
6. Serve immediately as a refreshing and flavorful Greek salad.

Nutritional Info (per serving): Calories: 220 | Fat: 18g | Carbs: 10g | Protein: 6g

Tip: For added protein, you can add grilled chicken or tofu to the salad.

Quinoa and Black Bean Salad

Prep: 15 mins | Cook: 15 mins | Serves: 4

Ingredients:
- 1 cup quinoa, rinsed (US & UK)
- 1 can (15 oz) black beans, drained and rinsed (US & UK)
- 1 red bell pepper, diced (US & UK)
- 1/2 cup corn kernels (fresh, canned, or frozen) (US & UK)
- 1/4 cup chopped fresh cilantro (US & UK)
- 2 tablespoons lime juice (US & UK)
- 2 tablespoons extra virgin olive oil (US & UK)
- 1 teaspoon ground cumin (US & UK)
- Salt and pepper, to taste
- Optional garnish: avocado slices, lime wedges

Instructions:
1. In a saucepan, combine quinoa and 2 cups of water. Bring to a boil, then reduce heat, cover, and simmer for 1215 minutes until quinoa is cooked and water is absorbed.
2. Fluff the cooked quinoa with a fork and let it cool slightly.
3. In a large bowl, combine cooked quinoa, black beans, diced red bell pepper, corn kernels, and chopped fresh cilantro.
4. In a small bowl, whisk together lime juice, extra virgin olive oil, ground cumin, salt, and pepper to make the dressing.
5. Pour the dressing over the salad ingredients and toss until well combined.
6. Serve the quinoa and black bean salad at room temperature or chilled.
7. Garnish with avocado slices and lime wedges, if desired.

Nutritional Info (per serving): Calories: 300 | Fat: 10g | Carbs: 45g | Protein: 10g

Tip: You can add diced tomatoes or jalapenos for extra flavor and spice.

Kale and Brussels Sprouts Salad

Prep: 15 mins | Cook: 0 mins | Serves: 4

Ingredients:
- 4 cups kale leaves, stems removed and thinly sliced (US & UK)
- 2 cups Brussels sprouts, trimmed and thinly sliced (US & UK)
- 1/4 cup dried cranberries (US & UK)
- 1/4 cup sliced almonds, toasted (US & UK)
- 1/4 cup grated Parmesan cheese (US & UK)
- 2 tablespoons lemon juice (US & UK)
- 2 tablespoons extra virgin olive oil (US & UK)
- 1 tablespoon honey (US & UK)
- Salt and pepper, to taste

Instructions:
1. In a large bowl, combine thinly sliced kale leaves and Brussels sprouts.
2. In a small bowl, whisk together lemon juice, extra virgin olive oil, honey, salt, and pepper to make the dressing.
3. Pour the dressing over the kale and Brussels sprouts mixture and toss until well coated.
4. Add dried cranberries, toasted sliced almonds, and grated Parmesan cheese to the salad and toss to combine.
5. Serve the kale and Brussels sprouts salad immediately as a nutritious and flavorful side dish or light meal.

Nutritional Info (per serving): Calories: 250 | Fat: 15g | Carbs: 25g | Protein: 8g

Tip: Massaging the kale leaves with a bit of olive oil and lemon juice before adding other ingredients helps to soften the leaves and enhance flavor.

Cobb Salad

Prep: 20 mins | Cook: 15 mins | Serves: 4

Ingredients:
- 4 cups mixed salad greens (US & UK)
- 2 boneless, skinless chicken breasts, grilled and sliced (US & UK)
- 4 slices bacon, cooked and crumbled (US & UK)
- 2 hardboiled eggs, sliced (US & UK)
- 1 avocado, diced (US & UK)
- 1 cup cherry tomatoes, halved (US & UK)
- 1/2 cup crumbled blue cheese (US & UK)
- 1/4 cup sliced green onions (US & UK)
- Salt and pepper, to taste
- Optional dressing: balsamic vinaigrette or ranch dressing

Instructions:
1. In a large salad bowl, arrange mixed salad greens as the base.
2. Arrange grilled and sliced chicken breasts, cooked and crumbled bacon, sliced hardboiled eggs, diced avocado, halved cherry tomatoes, crumbled blue cheese, and sliced green onions on top of the salad greens in rows.
3. Season with salt and pepper to taste.
4. Drizzle with your choice of dressing, such as balsamic vinaigrette or ranch dressing, or serve the dressing on the side.
5. Toss the salad gently just before serving to combine the ingredients and distribute the dressing evenly.
6. Serve the Cobb salad immediately as a satisfying and wholesome meal option.

Nutritional Info (per serving): Calories: 350 | Fat: 20g | Carbs: 15g | Protein: 30g

Tip: You can customize the Cobb salad by adding or omitting ingredients according to your preference, such as grilled corn, diced cucumber, or black olives.

Taco Salad

Prep: 20 mins | Cook: 10 mins | Serves: 4

Ingredients:
- 1 lb lean ground turkey or beef (US & UK)
- 1 packet taco seasoning mix (US & UK)
- 4 cups shredded lettuce (US & UK)
- 1 cup diced tomatoes (US & UK)
- 1 cup canned black beans, drained and rinsed (US & UK)
- 1 cup corn kernels (fresh, canned, or frozen) (US & UK)
- 1/2 cup shredded cheddar cheese (US & UK)
- 1/4 cup sliced black olives (US & UK)
- 1/4 cup chopped fresh cilantro (US & UK)
- 1 avocado, diced (US & UK)
- Optional toppings: salsa, sour cream, tortilla strips

Instructions:
1. In a skillet, cook ground turkey or beef over medium heat until browned. Drain excess fat.
2. Add taco seasoning mix to the cooked meat according to package instructions. Stir to combine and simmer for 5 minutes.
3. In a large salad bowl, layer shredded lettuce as the base.
4. Arrange seasoned meat, diced tomatoes, black beans, corn kernels, shredded cheddar cheese, sliced black olives, chopped fresh cilantro, and diced avocado on top of the lettuce.
5. Serve the taco salad with optional toppings like salsa, sour cream, and tortilla strips on the side.
6. Toss the salad just before serving to combine the ingredients and distribute the toppings evenly.
7. Enjoy the taco salad immediately as a flavorful and satisfying meal option.

Nutritional Info (per serving): Calories: 350 | Fat: 15g | Carbs: 25g | Protein: 25g

Tip: You can use leftover cooked chicken or beef instead of ground meat to save time.

Caprese Salad

Prep: 10 mins | Cook: 0 mins | Serves: 4

Ingredients:
- 4 large tomatoes, sliced (US & UK)
- 8 oz fresh mozzarella cheese, sliced (US & UK)
- Fresh basil leaves (US & UK)
- Extra virgin olive oil (US & UK)
- Balsamic glaze (US & UK)
- Salt and pepper, to taste

Instructions:
1. Arrange tomato slices and fresh mozzarella cheese slices alternately on a serving platter.
2. Tuck fresh basil leaves between the tomato and mozzarella slices.
3. Drizzle extra virgin olive oil and balsamic glaze over the salad.
4. Season with salt and pepper to taste.
5. Serve the Caprese salad immediately as a simple yet elegant appetizer or side dish.

Nutritional Info (per serving): Calories: 250 | Fat: 18g | Carbs: 8g | Protein: 15g

Tip: You can sprinkle the salad with a pinch of dried oregano or freshly ground black pepper for extra flavor.

Arugula Salad with Roasted Beets

Prep: 15 mins | Cook: 40 mins | Serves: 4

Ingredients:
- 4 medium beets, peeled and diced (US & UK)
- 6 cups arugula (US & UK)
- 1/4 cup crumbled goat cheese (US & UK)
- 1/4 cup chopped walnuts, toasted (US & UK)
- 2 tablespoons balsamic vinegar (US & UK)
- 1 tablespoon honey (US & UK)
- 2 tablespoons extra virgin olive oil (US & UK)
- Salt and pepper, to taste

Instructions:
1. Preheat your air fryer to 375°F (190°C) for 3 minutes. [Function used: Preheat]
2. Place diced beets in the air fryer basket and air fry for 3040 minutes until tender and slightly caramelized. [Function used: Air frying]
3. In a small bowl, whisk together balsamic vinegar, honey, extra virgin olive oil, salt, and pepper to make the dressing.
4. In a large salad bowl, combine arugula, roasted beets, crumbled goat cheese, and toasted chopped walnuts.
5. Drizzle the dressing over the salad ingredients and toss until well coated.
6. Serve the arugula salad with roasted beets immediately as a flavorful and nutritious dish.

Nutritional Info (per serving): Calories: 200 | Fat: 14g | Carbs: 18g | Protein: 6g

Tip: You can roast the beets in advance and store them in the refrigerator for quick assembly of the salad.

Southwest Chicken Salad

Prep: 20 mins | Cook: 10 mins | Serves: 4

Ingredients:
- 2 boneless, skinless chicken breasts, grilled and sliced (US & UK)
- 4 cups mixed salad greens (US & UK)
- 1 cup cherry tomatoes, halved (US & UK)
- 1/2 cup canned black beans, drained and rinsed (US & UK)
- 1/2 cup corn kernels (fresh, canned, or frozen) (US & UK)
- 1/4 cup shredded cheddar cheese (US & UK)
- 1/4 cup sliced black olives (US & UK)
- 1/4 cup chopped fresh cilantro (US & UK)
- 1 avocado, diced (US & UK)
- 1/4 cup salsa (US & UK)
- 1/4 cup sour cream (US & UK)

Instructions:
1. In a large salad bowl, arrange mixed salad greens as the base.
2. Arrange grilled and sliced chicken breasts, halved cherry tomatoes, drained and rinsed black beans, corn kernels, shredded cheddar cheese, sliced black olives, chopped fresh cilantro, and diced avocado on top of the salad greens.
3. Drizzle salsa and sour cream over the salad.
4. Serve the Southwest chicken salad immediately as a delicious and satisfying meal option.

Nutritional Info (per serving): Calories: 350 | Fat: 15g | Carbs: 25g | Protein: 30g

Tip: You can add tortilla strips or crushed tortilla chips for extra crunch and texture.

LemonHerb Chicken Salad

Prep: 15 mins | Cook: 20 mins | Serves: 4

Ingredients:
- 2 boneless, skinless chicken breasts (US & UK)
- 2 tablespoons olive oil (US & UK)
- 2 tablespoons lemon juice (US & UK)
- 1 teaspoon dried thyme (US & UK)
- 1 teaspoon dried rosemary (US & UK)
- Salt and pepper, to taste
- 4 cups mixed salad greens (US & UK)
- 1 cup cherry tomatoes, halved (US & UK)
- 1 cucumber, sliced (US & UK)
- 1/4 cup sliced red onion (US & UK)
- 1/4 cup crumbled feta cheese (US & UK)
- Optional dressing: lemon vinaigrette

Instructions:
1. Preheat your air fryer to 375°F (190°C) for 3 minutes. [Function used: Preheat]
2. In a small bowl, whisk together olive oil, lemon juice, dried thyme, dried rosemary, salt, and pepper to create a marinade.
3. Place chicken breasts in a shallow dish and pour the marinade over them, ensuring they are evenly coated. Let them marinate for 1015 minutes.
4. Place marinated chicken breasts in the air fryer basket.
5. Air fry at 375°F (190°C) for 1520 minutes, flipping halfway through, until the chicken is cooked through and reaches an internal temperature of 165°F (74°C). [Function used: Air frying]
6. Remove the chicken from the air fryer and let it rest for a few minutes before slicing.
7. In a large salad bowl, arrange mixed salad greens as the base.
8. Top the salad greens with sliced cherry tomatoes, sliced cucumber, sliced red onion, and crumbled feta cheese.
9. Slice the cooked lemonherb chicken and arrange it on top of the salad.
10. Serve the lemonherb chicken salad with your choice of dressing, such as lemon vinaigrette, on the side.

Nutritional Info (per serving): Calories: 250 | Fat: 12g | Carbs: 10g | Protein: 25g

Tip: You can customize the salad by adding additional vegetables or herbs to suit your taste preferences.

CHAPTER 5: VEGETARIAN MAINS

Cauliflower Steaks with Chimichurri Sauce

Prep: 15 mins | Cook: 20 mins | Serves: 2

Ingredients:
- ✓ 1 large cauliflower head, sliced into steaks (US & UK)
- ✓ 2 tablespoons olive oil (US & UK)
- ✓ Salt and pepper, to taste
- ✓ For Chimichurri Sauce:
- ✓ 1/2 cup fresh parsley, finely chopped (US & UK)
- ✓ 2 cloves garlic, minced (US & UK)
- ✓ 2 tablespoons red wine vinegar (US & UK)
- ✓ 1/4 cup extra virgin olive oil (US & UK)
- ✓ Salt and pepper, to taste
- ✓ Optional garnish: lemon wedges

Instructions:
1. Preheat your air fryer to 375°F (190°C) for 3 minutes. [Function used: Preheat]
2. Brush both sides of cauliflower steaks with olive oil and season with salt and pepper.
3. Place cauliflower steaks in the air fryer basket in a single layer.
4. Air fry for 1012 minutes, flipping halfway through, until golden brown and tender. [Function used: Air frying]
5. While the cauliflower cooks, prepare the chimichurri sauce. In a bowl, combine finely chopped parsley, minced garlic, red wine vinegar, extra virgin olive oil, salt, and pepper. Mix well.
6. Serve the cauliflower steaks hot with chimichurri sauce drizzled on top.
7. Garnish with lemon wedges, if desired.

Nutritional Info (per serving): Calories: 180 | Fat: 14g | Carbs: 12g | Protein: 4g

Tip: For extra flavor, sprinkle smoked paprika or chili powder on the cauliflower steaks before air frying.

Stuffed Portobello Mushrooms

Prep: 15 mins | Cook: 15 mins | Serves: 2

Ingredients:
- 2 large Portobello mushrooms, stems removed (US & UK)
- 1 tablespoon olive oil (US & UK)
- 2 cloves garlic, minced (US & UK)
- 1/2 cup baby spinach, chopped (US & UK)
- 1/4 cup sundried tomatoes, chopped (US & UK)
- 1/4 cup feta cheese, crumbled (US & UK)
- Salt and pepper, to taste
- Optional garnish: fresh parsley

Instructions:
1. Preheat your air fryer to 375°F (190°C) for 3 minutes. [Function used: Preheat]
2. In a skillet, heat olive oil over medium heat. Add minced garlic and sauté until fragrant.
3. Add chopped baby spinach and sundried tomatoes to the skillet. Cook until spinach wilts.
4. Season with salt and pepper, then remove from heat.
5. Place Portobello mushrooms in the air fryer basket.
6. Spoon the spinach and sundried tomato mixture into the mushroom caps.
7. Top each mushroom with crumbled feta cheese.
8. Air fry for 10-12 minutes until mushrooms are tender and cheese is melted. [Function used: Air frying]
9. Garnish with fresh parsley before serving.

Nutritional Info (per serving): Calories: 120 | Fat: 8g | Carbs: 10g | Protein: 5g

Tip: You can customize the filling by adding ingredients like diced bell peppers or cooked quinoa.

Vegetable Frittata

Prep: 15 mins | Cook: 20 mins | Serves: 4

Ingredients:
- 6 large eggs (US & UK)
- 1/4 cup milk (US & UK)
- 1 tablespoon olive oil (US & UK)
- 1 small onion, diced (US & UK)
- 1 bell pepper, diced (US & UK)
- 1 cup baby spinach (US & UK)
- 1/2 cup cherry tomatoes, halved (US & UK)
- Salt and pepper, to taste
- Optional addins: grated cheese, diced mushrooms

Instructions:
1. Preheat your air fryer to 350°F (175°C) for 3 minutes. [Function used: Preheat]
2. In a bowl, whisk together eggs, milk, salt, and pepper until well combined.
3. Heat olive oil in a skillet over medium heat. Add diced onion and bell pepper, and sauté until softened.
4. Add baby spinach and halved cherry tomatoes to the skillet. Cook until spinach wilts and tomatoes soften.
5. Pour the egg mixture into the skillet over the vegetables.
6. Cook for 34 minutes until the edges start to set.
7. Transfer the skillet to the air fryer basket.
8. Air fry for 1012 minutes until the frittata is set and golden brown on top. [Function used: Air frying]
9. Let the frittata cool slightly before slicing and serving.

Nutritional Info (per serving): Calories: 160 | Fat: 10g | Carbs: 8g | Protein: 10g

Tip: Feel free to use any combination of vegetables and herbs you like for your frittata.

Lentil and Sweet Potato Shepherd's Pie

Prep: 20 mins | Cook: 25 mins | Serves: 4

Ingredients:
- ✓ 2 medium sweet potatoes, peeled and diced (US & UK)
- ✓ 1 cup green lentils, cooked (US & UK)
- ✓ 1 tablespoon olive oil (US & UK)
- ✓ 1 small onion, diced (US & UK)
- ✓ 1 carrot, diced (US & UK)
- ✓ 2 cloves garlic, minced (US & UK)
- ✓ 1 celery stalk, diced (US & UK)
- ✓ 1 cup vegetable broth (US & UK)
- ✓ 1 teaspoon dried thyme (US & UK)
- ✓ Salt and pepper, to taste
- ✓ Optional topping: grated cheese

Instructions:
1. Preheat your air fryer to 375°F (190°C) for 3 minutes. [Function used: Preheat]
2. Place diced sweet potatoes in the air fryer basket.
3. Air fry for 1518 minutes until sweet potatoes are tender and lightly browned. [Function used: Air frying]
4. In a skillet, heat olive oil over medium heat. Add diced onion and minced garlic, and sauté until fragrant.
5. Add diced carrot and celery to the skillet. Cook until vegetables are softened.
6. Stir in cooked green lentils, vegetable broth, dried thyme, salt, and pepper. Simmer for 57 minutes until the mixture thickens.
7. Transfer the lentil and vegetable mixture to an ovensafe dish.
8. Arrange the airfried sweet potatoes on top of the lentil mixture.
9. Optional: Sprinkle grated cheese over the sweet potatoes.
10. Broil in the air fryer for 57 minutes until the cheese is melted and bubbly. [Function used: Broil]
11. Let the shepherd's pie cool slightly before serving.

Nutritional Info (per serving): Calories: 280 | Fat: 5g | Carbs: 50g | Protein: 10g

Tip: You can use mashed cauliflower instead of sweet potatoes for a lowercarb option.

Quinoa Stuffed Bell Peppers

Prep: 20 mins | Cook: 25 mins | Serves: 4

Ingredients:
- ✓ 4 large bell peppers, halved and seeded (US & UK)
- ✓ 1 cup quinoa, cooked (US & UK)
- ✓ 1 tablespoon olive oil (US & UK)
- ✓ 1 small onion, diced (US & UK)
- ✓ 2 cloves garlic, minced (US & UK)
- ✓ 1 zucchini, diced (US & UK)
- ✓ 1 cup canned black beans, drained and rinsed (US & UK)
- ✓ 1 cup cherry tomatoes, halved (US & UK)
- ✓ 1 teaspoon ground cumin (US & UK)
- ✓ Salt and pepper, to taste
- ✓ Optional topping: shredded cheese

Instructions:
1. Preheat your air fryer to 375°F (190°C) for 3 minutes. [Function used: Preheat]
2. In a skillet, heat olive oil over medium heat. Add diced onion and minced garlic, and sauté until softened.
3. Add diced zucchini to the skillet. Cook until tender.
4. Stir in cooked quinoa, drained black beans, cherry tomatoes, ground cumin, salt, and pepper. Cook for 34 minutes until heated through.
5. Spoon the quinoa mixture into halved bell peppers, pressing down gently to pack the filling.
6. Place stuffed bell peppers in the air fryer basket.
7. Air fry for 1518 minutes until bell peppers are tender and filling is heated through. [Function used: Air frying]
8. Optional: Sprinkle shredded cheese over the stuffed bell peppers during the last 5 minutes of cooking.
9. Let the quinoastuffed bell peppers cool slightly before serving.

Nutritional Info (per serving): Calories: 280 | Fat: 5g | Carbs: 45g | Protein: 10g

Tip: You can customize the filling by adding ingredients like corn, diced carrots, or diced mushrooms.

Veggie Burgers

Prep: 15 mins | Cook: 15 mins | Serves: 4

Ingredients:
- 1 can (15 oz) black beans, drained and rinsed (US & UK)
- 1/2 cup cooked quinoa (US & UK)
- 1/2 cup rolled oats (US & UK)
- 1/4 cup grated carrot (US & UK)
- 1/4 cup finely chopped onion (US & UK)
- 2 cloves garlic, minced (US & UK)
- 1 teaspoon ground cumin (US & UK)
- 1 teaspoon smoked paprika (US & UK)
- Salt and pepper, to taste
- 1 tablespoon olive oil (US & UK)
- Burger buns and toppings of your choice

Instructions:
1. Preheat your air fryer to 375°F (190°C) for 3 minutes. [Function used: Preheat]
2. In a bowl, mash black beans with a fork or potato masher until mostly smooth.
3. Add cooked quinoa, rolled oats, grated carrot, finely chopped onion, minced garlic, ground cumin, smoked paprika, salt, and pepper to the mashed black beans. Mix until well combined.
4. Divide the mixture into 4 portions and shape each portion into a burger patty.
5. Brush olive oil on both sides of each veggie burger patty.
6. Place veggie burger patties in the air fryer basket.
7. Air fry for 1215 minutes, flipping halfway through, until burgers are golden brown and cooked through. [Function used: Air frying]
8. Serve the veggie burgers on burger buns with your favorite toppings.

Nutritional Info (per serving, excluding bun and toppings): Calories: 220 | Fat: 5g | Carbs: 35g | Protein: 10g

Tip: You can freeze uncooked veggie burger patties for later use. Simply wrap them individually in plastic wrap and store in an airtight container.

Tofu StirFry

Prep: 15 mins | Cook: 15 mins | Serves: 4

Ingredients:
- 14 oz (400g) firm tofu, drained and cubed (US & UK)
- 2 tablespoons soy sauce (US & UK)
- 1 tablespoon hoisin sauce (US & UK)
- 1 tablespoon rice vinegar (US & UK)
- 1 tablespoon sesame oil (US & UK)
- 1 tablespoon olive oil (US & UK)
- 2 cloves garlic, minced (US & UK)
- 1 teaspoon grated ginger (US & UK)
- 1 bell pepper, sliced (US & UK)
- 1 carrot, julienned (US & UK)
- 1 cup broccoli florets (US & UK)
- 1 cup snow peas (US & UK)
- Cooked rice or noodles, for serving

Instructions:
1. Preheat your air fryer to 375°F (190°C) for 3 minutes. [Function used: Preheat]
2. In a bowl, mix together soy sauce, hoisin sauce, rice vinegar, and sesame oil to create the sauce.
3. Toss cubed tofu in the sauce mixture until evenly coated.
4. Place marinated tofu cubes in the air fryer basket.
5. Air fry for 1215 minutes, shaking the basket halfway through, until tofu is crispy and golden brown. [Function used: Air frying]
6. In a skillet, heat olive oil over medium heat. Add minced garlic and grated ginger, and sauté until fragrant.
7. Add sliced bell pepper, julienned carrot, broccoli florets, and snow peas to the skillet. Stirfry until vegetables are tendercrisp.
8. Add the airfried tofu cubes to the skillet and toss to combine with the vegetables.
9. Serve the tofu stirfry hot over cooked rice or noodles.

Nutritional Info (per serving, excluding rice or noodles): Calories: 180 | Fat: 10g | Carbs: 15g | Protein: 12g

Tip: Feel free to add other vegetables of your choice, such as mushrooms, baby corn, or water chestnuts, to the stirfry.

Eggplant Parmesan

Prep: 20 mins | Cook: 20 mins | Serves: 4

Ingredients:
- 1 large eggplant, sliced into rounds (US & UK)
- 1 cup marinara sauce (US & UK)
- 1/2 cup grated Parmesan cheese (US & UK)
- 1/2 cup shredded mozzarella cheese (US & UK)
- 1/4 cup breadcrumbs (US & UK)
- 1 teaspoon dried Italian herbs (US & UK)
- 1 tablespoon olive oil (US & UK)
- Fresh basil leaves, for garnish

Instructions:
1. Preheat your air fryer to 375°F (190°C) for 3 minutes. [Function used: Preheat]
2. In a shallow dish, mix together breadcrumbs and dried Italian herbs.
3. Dip eggplant slices in the breadcrumb mixture, coating both sides evenly.
4. Brush olive oil on both sides of each breaded eggplant slice.
5. Place breaded eggplant slices in the air fryer basket in a single layer.
6. Air fry for 1012 minutes, flipping halfway through, until eggplant slices are golden brown and tender. [Function used: Air frying]
7. Remove the airfried eggplant slices from the air fryer and top each slice with marinara sauce, grated Parmesan cheese, and shredded mozzarella cheese.
8. Return the topped eggplant slices to the air fryer basket.
9. Air fry for an additional 58 minutes until the cheese is melted and bubbly. [Function used: Air frying]
10. Garnish with fresh basil leaves before serving.

Nutritional Info (per serving): Calories: 200 | Fat: 10g | Carbs: 20g | Protein: 10g

Tip: You can serve eggplant Parmesan with cooked pasta or a side salad for a complete meal.

Zucchini Lasagna

Prep: 30 mins | Cook: 40 mins | Serves: 4

Ingredients:
- 2 large zucchini, sliced lengthwise into thin strips (US & UK)
- 1 cup marinara sauce (US & UK)
- 1 cup ricotta cheese (US & UK)
- 1/2 cup shredded mozzarella cheese (US & UK)
- 1/4 cup grated Parmesan cheese (US & UK)
- 1 egg, beaten (US & UK)
- 1 teaspoon dried Italian herbs (US & UK)
- Salt and pepper, to taste

Instructions:
1. Preheat your air fryer to 375°F (190°C) for 3 minutes. [Function used: Preheat]
2. In a bowl, combine ricotta cheese, shredded mozzarella cheese, grated Parmesan cheese, beaten egg, dried Italian herbs, salt, and pepper to create the cheese mixture.
3. Spread a thin layer of marinara sauce on the bottom of an ovensafe dish.
4. Arrange a layer of zucchini strips over the marinara sauce.
5. Spread a layer of the cheese mixture over the zucchini strips.
6. Repeat the layers of marinara sauce, zucchini strips, and cheese mixture until all ingredients are used, ending with a layer of cheese mixture on top.
7. Place the assembled lasagna in the air fryer basket.
8. Air fry for 3540 minutes until the zucchini is tender and the cheese is golden and bubbly. [Function used: Air frying]
9. Let the zucchini lasagna cool slightly before slicing and serving.

Nutritional Info (per serving): Calories: 220 | Fat: 15g | Carbs: 10g | Protein: 15g

Tip: You can add cooked spinach or mushrooms to the cheese mixture for extra flavor and nutrition

Chickpea Curry

Prep: 15 mins | Cook: 20 mins | Serves: 4

Ingredients:
- 2 tablespoons olive oil (US & UK)
- 1 onion, diced (US & UK)
- 2 cloves garlic, minced (US & UK)
- 1 tablespoon grated ginger (US & UK)
- 2 teaspoons curry powder (US & UK)
- 1 teaspoon ground cumin (US & UK)
- 1 teaspoon ground coriander (US & UK)
- 1/2 teaspoon turmeric powder (US & UK)
- 1/4 teaspoon cayenne pepper (optional) (US & UK)
- 1 can (15 oz) chickpeas, drained and rinsed (US & UK)
- 1 can (14 oz) diced tomatoes (US & UK)
- 1 can (14 oz) coconut milk (US & UK)
- Salt and pepper, to taste
- Fresh cilantro, for garnish
- Cooked rice or naan, for serving

Instructions:
1. Preheat your air fryer to 375°F (190°C) for 3 minutes. [Function used: Preheat]
2. In a skillet, heat olive oil over medium heat. Add diced onion and sauté until softened.
3. Add minced garlic and grated ginger to the skillet. Cook for another minute until fragrant.
4. Stir in curry powder, ground cumin, ground coriander, turmeric powder, and cayenne pepper (if using). Cook for 12 minutes to toast the spices.
5. Add drained chickpeas, diced tomatoes, and coconut milk to the skillet. Season with salt and pepper to taste.
6. Simmer the chickpea curry for 1015 minutes, stirring occasionally, until the flavors meld together and the sauce thickens slightly.
7. While the curry simmers, prepare your serving bowls with cooked rice or naan.
8. Once the curry is ready, taste and adjust seasoning if needed.
9. Serve the chickpea curry hot, garnished with fresh cilantro.

Nutritional Info (per serving, excluding rice or naan): Calories: 280 | Fat: 20g | Carbs: 25g | Protein: 6g

Tip: You can add diced vegetables like bell peppers, carrots, or spinach to the curry for added nutrition and flavor.

Vegetable Enchiladas

Prep: 20 mins | Cook: 25 mins | Serves: 4

Ingredients:
- 8 small corn tortillas (US & UK)
- 2 cups mixed vegetables (such as bell peppers, onions, zucchini), diced (US & UK)
- 1 cup black beans, cooked (US & UK)
- 1 cup enchilada sauce (storebought or homemade) (US & UK)
- 1 cup shredded cheese (cheddar, Monterey Jack, or Mexican blend) (US & UK)
- 1 tablespoon olive oil (US & UK)
- Salt and pepper, to taste
- Optional toppings: diced avocado, chopped cilantro, sour cream

Instructions:
1. Preheat your air fryer to 375°F (190°C) for 3 minutes. [Function used: Preheat]
2. In a skillet, heat olive oil over medium heat. Add diced mixed vegetables and cook until tendercrisp.
3. Season the vegetables with salt and pepper to taste.
4. Warm the corn tortillas in the microwave or on a skillet to make them pliable.
5. Spoon a portion of cooked vegetables and black beans onto each tortilla, then roll up tightly.
6. Place the rolled enchiladas seam side down in the air fryer basket.
7. Pour enchilada sauce over the top of the enchiladas, ensuring they are evenly coated.
8. Sprinkle shredded cheese over the enchiladas.
9. Air fry for 1520 minutes until the cheese is melted and bubbly, and the enchiladas are heated through. [Function used: Air frying]
10. Serve the vegetable enchiladas hot with optional toppings like diced avocado, chopped cilantro, and sour cream.

Nutritional Info (per serving): Calories: 320 | Fat: 12g | Carbs: 40g | Protein: 14g

Tip: You can customize the filling by adding ingredients like corn, diced tomatoes, or spinach.

Sweet Potato and Black Bean Burrito Bowls

Prep: 20 mins | Cook: 20 mins | Serves: 4

Ingredients:
- 2 large sweet potatoes, peeled and diced (US & UK)
- 1 tablespoon olive oil (US & UK)
- 1 teaspoon ground cumin (US & UK)
- 1 teaspoon chili powder (US & UK)
- Salt and pepper, to taste
- 1 can (15 oz) black beans, drained and rinsed (US & UK)
- 1 cup cooked quinoa (US & UK)
- 1 cup salsa (storebought or homemade) (US & UK)
- 1 avocado, sliced (US & UK)
- Optional toppings: shredded cheese, chopped cilantro, lime wedges

Instructions:
1. Preheat your air fryer to 375°F (190°C) for 3 minutes. [Function used: Preheat]
2. In a bowl, toss diced sweet potatoes with olive oil, ground cumin, chili powder, salt, and pepper until evenly coated.
3. Spread seasoned sweet potatoes in a single layer in the air fryer basket.
4. Air fry for 1520 minutes until sweet potatoes are tender and lightly browned. [Function used: Air frying]
5. In a separate skillet, heat black beans over medium heat until warmed through.
6. Assemble burrito bowls by dividing cooked quinoa, airfried sweet potatoes, and black beans among serving bowls.
7. Top each bowl with salsa and sliced avocado.
8. Optional: Sprinkle shredded cheese and chopped cilantro over the burrito bowls.
9. Serve the sweet potato and black bean burrito bowls hot, with lime wedges on the side.

Nutritional Info (per serving): Calories: 320 | Fat: 12g | Carbs: 45g | Protein: 10g

Tip: You can add additional toppings like diced tomatoes, shredded lettuce, or Greek yogurt for extra flavor.

Roasted Vegetable Medley

Prep: 15 mins | Cook: 20 mins | Serves: 4

Ingredients:
- ✓ 2 cups mixed vegetables (such as bell peppers, cherry tomatoes, broccoli, cauliflower), chopped (US & UK)
- ✓ 2 tablespoons olive oil (US & UK)
- ✓ 1 teaspoon dried Italian herbs (US & UK)
- ✓ Salt and pepper, to taste
- ✓ Optional: grated Parmesan cheese, balsamic glaze

Instructions:
1. Preheat your air fryer to 375°F (190°C) for 3 minutes. [Function used: Preheat]
2. In a large bowl, toss chopped mixed vegetables with olive oil, dried Italian herbs, salt, and pepper until well coated.
3. Spread seasoned vegetables in a single layer in the air fryer basket.
4. Air fry for 15-20 minutes until vegetables are tender and lightly browned, shaking the basket halfway through for even cooking. [Function used: Air frying]
5. Once cooked, transfer the roasted vegetable medley to a serving dish.
6. Optional: Sprinkle grated Parmesan cheese over the roasted vegetables before serving.
7. Drizzle with balsamic glaze for added flavor, if desired.
8. Serve the roasted vegetable medley hot as a side dish or as part of a main meal.

Nutritional Info (per serving): Calories: 120 | Fat: 8g | Carbs: 10g | Protein: 2g

Tip: Feel free to use your favorite vegetables or seasonal produce for this versatile dish.

Vegetarian Chili

Prep: 20 mins | Cook: 30 mins | Serves: 6

Ingredients:
- ✓ 1 tablespoon olive oil (US & UK)
- ✓ 1 onion, diced (US & UK)
- ✓ 2 cloves garlic, minced (US & UK)
- ✓ 1 bell pepper, diced (US & UK)
- ✓ 1 zucchini, diced (US & UK)
- ✓ 1 carrot, diced (US & UK)
- ✓ 1 can (15 oz) black beans, drained and rinsed (US & UK)
- ✓ 1 can (15 oz) kidney beans, drained and rinsed (US & UK)
- ✓ 1 can (14 oz) diced tomatoes (US & UK)
- ✓ 1 cup vegetable broth (US & UK)
- ✓ 2 tablespoons tomato paste (US & UK)
- ✓ 2 teaspoons chili powder (US & UK)
- ✓ 1 teaspoon ground cumin (US & UK)
- ✓ 1 teaspoon smoked paprika (US & UK)
- ✓ Salt and pepper, to taste
- ✓ Optional toppings: shredded cheese, chopped green onions, sour cream

Instructions:
1. Preheat your air fryer to 375°F (190°C) for 3 minutes. [Function used: Preheat]
2. In a skillet, heat olive oil over medium heat. Add diced onion and minced garlic, and sauté until softened.
3. Add diced bell pepper, zucchini, and carrot to the skillet. Cook until vegetables are tender.
4. Stir in drained black beans, kidney beans, diced tomatoes, vegetable broth, tomato paste, chili powder, ground cumin, smoked paprika, salt, and pepper. Bring the mixture to a simmer and let it cook for 1520 minutes, allowing the flavors to meld together and the chili to thicken.
5. While the chili simmers, preheat your air fryer to 375°F (190°C) for 3 minutes.
6. Once the chili is ready, transfer it to an ovensafe dish.
7. Place the dish in the air fryer basket and air fry for an additional 1015 minutes to further thicken the chili and intensify the flavors. [Function used: Air frying]
8. Serve the vegetarian chili hot, topped with shredded cheese, chopped green onions, and sour cream if desired.

Nutritional Info (per serving): Calories: 250 | Fat: 5g | Carbs: 40g | Protein: 12g

Tip: Adjust the spice level of the chili by adding more or less chili powder and smoked paprika according to your preference.

Baked Falafel with Tzatziki Sauce

Prep: 20 mins | Cook: 20 mins | Serves: 4

Ingredients:

For the Falafel:
- 1 can (15 oz) chickpeas, drained and rinsed (US & UK)
- 1/4 cup chopped fresh parsley (US & UK)
- 1/4 cup chopped fresh cilantro (US & UK)
- 1/4 cup chopped red onion (US & UK)
- 2 cloves garlic, minced (US & UK)
- 1 teaspoon ground cumin (US & UK)
- 1 teaspoon ground coriander (US & UK)
- 1/2 teaspoon baking powder (US & UK) and Salt and pepper, to taste
- 2 tablespoons olive oil (US & UK)
- **For the Tzatziki Sauce:**
- 1/2 cup Greek yogurt (US & UK)
- 1/4 cup grated cucumber, squeezed to remove excess moisture (US & UK)
- 1 tablespoon lemon juice (US & UK) and Salt and pepper, to taste
- 1 tablespoon chopped fresh dill (US & UK)
- Pita bread or lettuce leaves, for serving

Instructions:
1. Preheat your air fryer to 375°F (190°C) for 3 minutes. [Function used: Preheat]
2. In a food processor, combine chickpeas, chopped parsley, chopped cilantro, chopped red onion, minced garlic, ground cumin, ground coriander, baking powder, salt, and pepper. Pulse until the mixture comes together but still has some texture.
3. Shape the falafel mixture into small patties or balls.
4. Brush olive oil over the falafel patties or balls to coat evenly.
5. Place the falafel in the air fryer basket in a single layer.
6. Air fry for 1520 minutes, flipping halfway through, until falafel is golden brown and crispy. [Function used: Air frying]
7. While the falafel cooks, prepare the tzatziki sauce by combining Greek yogurt, grated cucumber, lemon juice, chopped fresh dill, salt, and pepper in a bowl. Mix well and refrigerate until ready to serve.
8. Serve the baked falafel hot, with tzatziki sauce on the side and pita bread or lettuce leaves for wrapping.

Nutritional Info (per serving, including tzatziki sauce): Calories: 220 | Fat: 10g | Carbs: 25g | Protein: 10g

Tip: You can customize the falafel by adding spices like paprika or cayenne pepper for extra flavor.

CHAPTER 6: POULTRY AND SEAFOOD

Cauliflower Steaks with Chimichurri Sauce

Prep: 15 mins | Cook: 20 mins | Serves: 2

Ingredients:
- 1 large cauliflower head, sliced into steaks (US & UK)
- 2 tablespoons olive oil (US & UK)
- Salt and pepper, to taste
- For Chimichurri Sauce:
- 1/2 cup fresh parsley, chopped (US & UK)
- 1/4 cup fresh cilantro, chopped (US & UK)
- 2 cloves garlic, minced (US & UK)
- 2 tablespoons red wine vinegar (US & UK)
- 1/4 cup olive oil (US & UK)
- Salt and pepper, to taste

Instructions:
1. Preheat your air fryer to 375°F (190°C) for 3 minutes. [Function used: Preheat]
2. Brush both sides of cauliflower steaks with olive oil and season with salt and pepper.
3. Place cauliflower steaks in the air fryer basket in a single layer.
4. Air fry for 10 minutes, flip the steaks, and air fry for an additional 10 minutes until golden brown and tender. [Function used: Air frying]
5. While the cauliflower cooks, prepare the chimichurri sauce by combining chopped parsley, chopped cilantro, minced garlic, red wine vinegar, olive oil, salt, and pepper in a bowl. Mix well.
6. Once the cauliflower steaks are cooked, transfer them to a serving plate and drizzle with chimichurri sauce.
7. Serve the cauliflower steaks hot, accompanied by additional chimichurri sauce on the side.

Nutritional Info (per serving): Calories: 250 | Fat: 20g | Carbs: 15g | Protein: 5g

Tip: You can sprinkle some crushed red pepper flakes over the cauliflower steaks for a spicy kick.

Stuffed Portobello Mushrooms

Prep: 15 mins | Cook: 15 mins | Serves: 2

Ingredients:
- 2 large Portobello mushrooms (US & UK)
- 1/2 cup spinach, chopped (US & UK)
- 1/4 cup sundried tomatoes, chopped (US & UK)
- 1/4 cup feta cheese, crumbled (US & UK)
- 2 tablespoons olive oil (US & UK)
- Salt and pepper, to taste
- Optional: balsamic glaze, for drizzling

Instructions:
1. Preheat your air fryer to 375°F (190°C) for 3 minutes. [Function used: Preheat]
2. Remove the stems from Portobello mushrooms and gently scrape out the gills.
3. In a bowl, mix chopped spinach, sundried tomatoes, and crumbled feta cheese.
4. Brush the outside of Portobello mushrooms with olive oil and season with salt and pepper.
5. Stuff each mushroom cap with the spinach, sundried tomato, and feta mixture.
6. Place stuffed mushrooms in the air fryer basket.
7. Air fry for 1215 minutes until mushrooms are tender and filling is heated through. [Function used: Air frying]
8. Once cooked, drizzle stuffed mushrooms with balsamic glaze if desired.
9. Serve the stuffed Portobello mushrooms hot as a flavorful appetizer or side dish.

Nutritional Info (per serving): Calories: 180 | Fat: 12g | Carbs: 10g | Protein: 8g

Tip: You can add cooked quinoa or couscous to the stuffing mixture for added texture and protein.

Vegetable Frittata

Prep: 10 mins | Cook: 20 mins | Serves: 4

Ingredients:
- 6 large eggs (US & UK)
- 1/4 cup milk (US & UK)
- 1 cup mixed vegetables (such as bell peppers, onions, spinach), diced (US & UK)
- 1/2 cup shredded cheese (cheddar, mozzarella, or feta) (US & UK)
- 1 tablespoon olive oil (US & UK)
- Salt and pepper, to taste

Instructions:
1. Preheat your air fryer to 350°F (175°C) for 3 minutes. [Function used: Preheat]
2. In a bowl, whisk together eggs and milk. Season with salt and pepper.
3. Heat olive oil in a skillet over medium heat. Add diced mixed vegetables and cook until softened.
4. Pour the egg mixture over the cooked vegetables in the skillet.
5. Sprinkle shredded cheese evenly over the top of the egg mixture.
6. Carefully transfer the skillet to the air fryer basket.
7. Air fry for 1520 minutes until the frittata is set in the center and lightly golden on top. [Function used: Air frying]
8. Once cooked, let the frittata cool slightly before slicing into wedges.
9. Serve the vegetable frittata warm or at room temperature for a delicious breakfast or brunch option.

Nutritional Info (per serving): Calories: 200 | Fat: 14g | Carbs: 6g | Protein: 14g

Tip: You can customize the frittata by adding your favorite vegetables or herbs.

Lentil and Sweet Potato Shepherd's Pie

Prep: 20 mins | Cook: 30 mins | Serves: 4

Ingredients:
- ✓ 2 cups cooked lentils (US & UK)
- ✓ 2 cups mashed sweet potatoes (US & UK)
- ✓ 1 onion, diced (US & UK)
- ✓ 2 cloves garlic, minced (US & UK)
- ✓ 1 carrot, diced (US & UK)
- ✓ 1 celery stalk, diced (US & UK)
- ✓ 1 cup frozen peas (US & UK)
- ✓ 1 cup vegetable broth (US & UK)
- ✓ 2 tablespoons tomato paste (US & UK)
- ✓ 1 tablespoon olive oil (US & UK)
- ✓ 1 teaspoon dried thyme (US & UK)
- ✓ Salt and pepper, to taste

Instructions:
1. Preheat your air fryer to 375°F (190°C) for 3 minutes. [Function used: Preheat]
2. Heat olive oil in a skillet over medium heat. Add diced onion, minced garlic, diced carrot, and diced celery. Cook until softened.
3. Stir in tomato paste and dried thyme. Cook for another minute.
4. Add cooked lentils, frozen peas, and vegetable broth to the skillet. Season with salt and pepper to taste. Simmer for 57 minutes until the mixture thickens slightly.
5. Transfer the lentil and vegetable mixture to an ovensafe dish.
6. Spread mashed sweet potatoes evenly over the top of the lentil mixture.
7. Place the dish in the air fryer basket.
8. Air fry for 2025 minutes until the shepherd's pie is heated through and the sweet potato topping is golden brown. [Function used: Air frying]
9. Once cooked, let the shepherd's pie cool slightly before serving.
10. Serve the lentil and sweet potato shepherd's pie hot, garnished with fresh herbs if desired.

Nutritional Info (per serving): Calories: 320 | Fat: 6g | Carbs: 55g | Protein: 12g

Tip: Feel free to add other vegetables like mushrooms or bell peppers to the lentil mixture for extra flavor and nutrition.

QuinoaStuffed Bell Peppers

Prep: 15 mins | Cook: 25 mins | Serves: 4

Ingredients:
- ✓ 4 large bell peppers (any color) (US & UK)
- ✓ 1 cup cooked quinoa (US & UK)
- ✓ 1 cup black beans, cooked (US & UK)
- ✓ 1 cup corn kernels (fresh, frozen, or canned) (US & UK)
- ✓ 1 cup diced tomatoes (US & UK)
- ✓ 1/2 cup shredded cheese (cheddar, Monterey Jack, or Mexican blend) (US & UK)
- ✓ 1 teaspoon ground cumin (US & UK)
- ✓ 1 teaspoon chili powder (US & UK)
- ✓ Salt and pepper, to taste
- ✓ Fresh cilantro, for garnish

Instructions:
1. Preheat your air fryer to 375°F (190°C) for 3 minutes. [Function used: Preheat]
2. Cut the tops off the bell peppers and remove the seeds and membranes.
3. In a bowl, mix together cooked quinoa, black beans, corn kernels, diced tomatoes, shredded cheese, ground cumin, chili powder, salt, and pepper.
4. Stuff each bell pepper with the quinoa mixture, pressing down gently to pack it in.
5. Place stuffed bell peppers in the air fryer basket.
6. Air fry for 2025 minutes until bell peppers are tender and filling is heated through. [Function used: Air frying]
7. Once cooked, remove the stuffed bell peppers from the air fryer and let them cool slightly.
8. Garnish with fresh cilantro before serving.

Nutritional Info (per serving): Calories: 280 | Fat: 7g | Carbs: 45g | Protein: 12g

Tip: You can customize the filling by adding ingredients like diced onions, garlic, or jalapenos for extra flavor.

Veggie Burgers

Prep: 20 mins | Cook: 15 mins | Serves: 4

Ingredients:
- 1 can (15 oz) black beans, drained and rinsed (US & UK)
- 1 cup cooked quinoa (US & UK)
- 1/2 cup rolled oats (US & UK)
- 1/2 cup shredded carrots (US & UK)
- 1/4 cup diced red onion (US & UK)
- 2 cloves garlic, minced (US & UK)
- 1 teaspoon ground cumin (US & UK)
- 1 teaspoon smoked paprika (US & UK)
- Salt and pepper, to taste
- 1 tablespoon olive oil (US & UK)

Instructions:
1. Preheat your air fryer to 375°F (190°C) for 3 minutes. [Function used: Preheat]
2. In a food processor, combine black beans, cooked quinoa, rolled oats, shredded carrots, diced red onion, minced garlic, ground cumin, smoked paprika, salt, and pepper. Pulse until mixture comes together but still has some texture.
3. Divide the mixture into 4 equal portions and shape each portion into a patty.
4. Brush both sides of each veggie burger patty with olive oil.
5. Place the veggie burger patties in the air fryer basket in a single layer.
6. Air fry for 1215 minutes, flipping halfway through, until burgers are golden brown and heated through. [Function used: Air frying]
7. Once cooked, remove the veggie burgers from the air fryer and let them cool slightly.
8. Serve the veggie burgers on buns with your favorite toppings and condiments.

Nutritional Info (per serving, excluding bun and toppings): Calories: 220 | Fat: 6g | Carbs: 35g | Protein: 10g

Tip: You can freeze uncooked veggie burger patties for later use. Just thaw before air frying.

Tofu StirFry

Prep: 15 mins | Cook: 15 mins | Serves: 4

Ingredients:
- 14 oz (400g) firm tofu, drained and cubed (US & UK)
- 2 cups mixed vegetables (such as bell peppers, broccoli, snap peas) (US & UK)
- 1 tablespoon soy sauce (US & UK)
- 1 tablespoon hoisin sauce (US & UK)
- 1 tablespoon sesame oil (US & UK)
- 2 cloves garlic, minced (US & UK)
- 1 teaspoon ginger, minced (US & UK)
- 2 green onions, chopped (US & UK)
- Cooked rice or noodles, for serving (optional)

Instructions:
1. Preheat your air fryer to 375°F (190°C) for 3 minutes. [Function used: Preheat]
2. In a bowl, toss cubed tofu with soy sauce, hoisin sauce, minced garlic, and minced ginger until evenly coated.
3. Place marinated tofu in the air fryer basket in a single layer.
4. Air fry for 1215 minutes until tofu is crispy and golden brown. [Function used: Air frying]
5. While the tofu cooks, heat sesame oil in a skillet over medium heat. Add mixed vegetables and stirfry until tendercrisp.
6. Add cooked tofu to the skillet with vegetables and toss to combine.
7. Stir in chopped green onions and cook for an additional minute.
8. Serve the tofu stirfry hot over cooked rice or noodles if desired.

Nutritional Info (per serving, excluding rice or noodles): Calories: 180 | Fat: 10g | Carbs: 12g | Protein: 15g

Tip: You can customize the stirfry by adding your favorite vegetables or adjusting the sauce to your taste.

Eggplant Parmesan

Prep: 20 mins | Cook: 25 mins | Serves: 4

Ingredients:
- 1 large eggplant, sliced into rounds (US & UK)
- 1/2 cup breadcrumbs (US & UK)
- 1/4 cup grated Parmesan cheese (US & UK)
- 1 teaspoon dried oregano (US & UK)
- 1 teaspoon dried basil (US & UK)
- 1/2 teaspoon garlic powder (US & UK)
- 1/2 teaspoon salt (US & UK)
- 1/4 teaspoon black pepper (US & UK)
- 2 eggs, beaten (US & UK)
- Marinara sauce (storebought or homemade) (US & UK)
- 1 cup shredded mozzarella cheese (US & UK)
- Fresh basil leaves, for garnish (optional)

Instructions:
1. Preheat your air fryer to 375°F (190°C) for 3 minutes. [Function used: Preheat]
2. In a shallow dish, mix breadcrumbs, grated Parmesan cheese, dried oregano, dried basil, garlic powder, salt, and black pepper.
3. Dip eggplant slices into beaten eggs, then coat evenly with breadcrumb mixture.
4. Place breaded eggplant slices in the air fryer basket in a single layer.
5. Air fry for 1012 minutes, flipping halfway through, until eggplant is golden and crispy. [Function used: Air frying]
6. Preheat your oven to 375°F (190°C).
7. In a baking dish, spread a thin layer of marinara sauce.
8. Arrange cooked eggplant slices in the baking dish, overlapping slightly.
9. Top each eggplant slice with additional marinara sauce and shredded mozzarella cheese.
10. Bake in the preheated oven for 1015 minutes until cheese is melted and bubbly.
11. Garnish with fresh basil leaves before serving.

Nutritional Info (per serving): Calories: 220 | Fat: 10g | Carbs: 20g | Protein: 12g

Tip: Serve eggplant Parmesan with a side of pasta or a fresh salad for a complete meal.

Zucchini Lasagna

Prep: 20 mins | Cook: 45 mins | Serves: 6

Ingredients:
- 2 large zucchinis, thinly sliced lengthwise (US & UK)
- 2 cups marinara sauce (storebought or homemade) (US & UK)
- 1 cup ricotta cheese (US & UK)
- 1 cup shredded mozzarella cheese (US & UK)
- 1/4 cup grated Parmesan cheese (US & UK)
- 1 egg (US & UK)
- 1 teaspoon dried oregano (US & UK)
- 1 teaspoon dried basil (US & UK)
- Salt and pepper, to taste
- Fresh basil leaves, for garnish (optional)

Instructions:
1. Preheat your air fryer to 375°F (190°C) for 3 minutes. [Function used: Preheat]
2. In a bowl, combine ricotta cheese, shreddedmozzarella cheese, grated Parmesan cheese, egg, dried oregano, dried basil, salt, and pepper. Mix until well combined.
3. In a separate bowl, spread a thin layer of marinara sauce on the bottom of your air fryersafe baking dish.
4. Arrange a layer of sliced zucchini on top of the marinara sauce.
5. Spread a layer of the ricotta cheese mixture over the zucchini slices.
6. Repeat layers of marinara sauce, zucchini slices, and ricotta cheese mixture until all ingredients are used, ending with a layer of marinara sauce on top.
7. Sprinkle the top layer with additional shredded mozzarella cheese and grated Parmesan cheese.
8. Cover the baking dish with aluminum foil.
9. Place the covered baking dish in the air fryer basket.
10. Air fry for 3035 minutes, then remove the foil and air fry for an additional 1015 minutes until lasagna is bubbly and cheese is golden brown. [Function used: Air frying]
11. Once cooked, let the zucchini lasagna cool for a few minutes before slicing.
12. Garnish with fresh basil leaves before serving.

Nutritional Info (per serving): Calories: 220 | Fat: 12g | Carbs: 12g | Protein: 16g

Tip: Letting the lasagna rest for 1015 minutes after cooking allows it to set, making it easier to slice and serve.

Chickpea Curry

Prep: 15 mins | Cook: 20 mins | Serves: 4

Ingredients:
- 2 cans (15 oz each) chickpeas, drained and rinsed (US & UK)
- 1 onion, diced (US & UK)
- 2 cloves garlic, minced (US & UK)
- 1 tablespoon curry powder (US & UK)
- 1 teaspoon ground cumin (US & UK)
- 1 teaspoon ground coriander (US & UK)
- 1/2 teaspoon turmeric (US & UK)
- 1/4 teaspoon cayenne pepper (optional, for heat) (US & UK)
- 1 can (14 oz) diced tomatoes (US & UK)
- 1 can (13.5 oz) coconut milk (US & UK)
- 1 tablespoon olive oil (US & UK)
- Salt and pepper, to taste
- Fresh cilantro, for garnish (optional)
- Cooked rice or naan bread, for serving

Instructions:
1. Preheat your air fryer to 375°F (190°C) for 3 minutes. [Function used: Preheat]
2. Heat olive oil in a skillet over medium heat. Add diced onion and minced garlic, and cook until softened.
3. Stir in curry powder, ground cumin, ground coriander, turmeric, and cayenne pepper (if using). Cook for another minute until fragrant.
4. Add drained chickpeas, diced tomatoes, and coconut milk to the skillet. Season with salt and pepper to taste. Simmer for 10-12 minutes until the curry thickens slightly.
5. Transfer the chickpea curry to an air fryer-safe baking dish.
6. Place the baking dish in the air fryer basket.
7. Air fry for 15-20 minutes until the curry is heated through and bubbling. [Function used: Air frying]
8. Once cooked, garnish the chickpea curry with fresh cilantro.
9. Serve the chickpea curry hot over cooked rice or with naan bread for a delicious meal.

Nutritional Info (per serving, excluding rice or naan bread): Calories: 280 | Fat: 15g | Carbs: 30g | Protein: 10g

Tip: Adjust the spice level of the curry by adding more or less cayenne pepper according to your preference.

Vegetable Enchiladas

Prep: 20 mins | Cook: 25 mins | Serves: 4

Ingredients:
- ✓ 8 small corn tortillas (US & UK)
- ✓ 2 cups mixed vegetables (such as bell peppers, onions, zucchini), diced (US & UK)
- ✓ 1 can (15 oz) black beans, drained and rinsed (US & UK)
- ✓ 1 cup enchilada sauce (storebought or homemade) (US & UK)
- ✓ 1 cup shredded cheese (cheddar, Monterey Jack, or Mexican blend) (US & UK)
- ✓ 2 tablespoons olive oil (US & UK)
- ✓ Salt and pepper, to taste
- ✓ Fresh cilantro, for garnish (optional)

Instructions:
1. Preheat your air fryer to 375°F (190°C) for 3 minutes. [Function used: Preheat]
2. In a skillet, heat olive oil over medium heat. Add diced mixed vegetables and cook until tendercrisp.
3. Stir in black beans and season with salt and pepper to taste. Cook for another 23 minutes until heated through.
4. Warm the corn tortillas in the microwave for a few seconds to make them pliable.
5. Place a spoonful of the vegetable and black bean mixture onto each tortilla. Roll up the tortillas and place them seamside down in an air fryersafe baking dish.
6. Pour enchilada sauce evenly over the rolled tortillas.
7. Sprinkle shredded cheese on top of the enchilada sauce.
8. Place the baking dish in the air fryer basket.
9. Air fry for 2025 minutes until the enchiladas are heated through and cheese is melted and bubbly. [Function used: Air frying]
10. Once cooked, let the enchiladas cool for a few minutes before serving.
11. Garnish with fresh cilantro before serving.

Nutritional Info (per serving): Calories: 320 | Fat: 15g | Carbs: 35g | Protein: 12g

Tip: Customize the enchiladas by adding ingredients like sliced jalapenos or diced tomatoes to the filling.

Sweet Potato and Black Bean Burrito Bowls

Prep: 20 mins | Cook: 25 mins | Serves: 4

Ingredients:
- 2 large sweet potatoes, peeled and cubed (US & UK)
- 1 can (15 oz) black beans, drained and rinsed (US & UK)
- 1 cup cooked quinoa (US & UK)
- 1 avocado, sliced (US & UK)
- 1/2 cup salsa (storebought or homemade) (US & UK)
- 1/4 cup Greek yogurt or sour cream (US & UK)
- 1/4 cup shredded cheese (cheddar, Monterey Jack, or Mexican blend) (US & UK)
- 2 tablespoons olive oil (US & UK)
- 1 teaspoon chili powder (US & UK)
- 1/2 teaspoon ground cumin (US & UK)
- Salt and pepper, to taste
- Fresh cilantro, for garnish (optional)

Instructions:
1. Preheat your air fryer to 375°F (190°C) for 3 minutes. [Function used: Preheat]
2. In a bowl, toss cubed sweet potatoes with olive oil, chili powder, ground cumin, salt, and pepper until evenly coated.
3. Place seasoned sweet potatoes in the air fryer basket in a single layer.
4. Air fry for 2025 minutes until sweet potatoes are tender and slightly crispy. [Function used: Air frying]
5. While the sweet potatoes cook, heat black beans and cooked quinoa in a saucepan over medium heat until heated through.
6. Divide cooked sweet potatoes, black beans, and quinoa among serving bowls.
7. Top each bowl with sliced avocado, salsa, Greek yogurt or sour cream, and shredded cheese.
8. Garnish with fresh cilantro before serving.

Nutritional Info (per serving): Calories: 380 | Fat: 15g | Carbs: 50g | Protein: 15g

Tip: Feel free to add additional toppings like sliced jalapenos, diced tomatoes, or shredded lettuce for extra flavor.

Roasted Vegetable Medley

Prep: 15 mins | Cook: 20 mins | Serves: 4

Ingredients:
- ✓ 2 cups mixed vegetables (such as bell peppers, onions, carrots, broccoli), diced (US & UK)
- ✓ 2 tablespoons olive oil (US & UK)
- ✓ 1 teaspoon dried thyme (US & UK)
- ✓ 1 teaspoon dried rosemary (US & UK)
- ✓ 1 teaspoon garlic powder (US & UK)
- ✓ Salt and pepper, to taste
- ✓ Fresh parsley, for garnish (optional)

Instructions:
1. Preheat your air fryer to 375°F (190°C) for 3 minutes. [Function used: Preheat]
2. In a bowl, toss diced mixed vegetables with olive oil, dried thyme, dried rosemary, garlic powder, salt, and pepper until evenly coated.
3. Place seasoned vegetables in the air fryer basket in a single layer.
4. Air fry for 1520 minutes until vegetables are tender and lightly browned, shaking the basket halfway through cooking. [Function used: Air frying]
5. Once cooked, transfer the roasted vegetable medley to a serving dish.
6. Garnish with fresh parsley before serving.

Nutritional Info (per serving): Calories: 120 | Fat: 7g | Carbs: 15g | Protein: 2g

Tip: You can use any combination of your favorite vegetables for this recipe.

Vegetarian Chili

Prep: 20 mins | Cook: 30 mins | Serves: 6

Ingredients:
- 1 can (15 oz) black beans, drained and rinsed (US & UK)
- 1 can (15 oz) kidney beans, drained and rinsed (US & UK)
- 1 can (15 oz) chickpeas, drained and rinsed (US & UK)
- 1 can (14 oz) diced tomatoes (US & UK)
- 1 onion, diced (US & UK)
- 2 cloves garlic, minced (US & UK)
- 1 bell pepper, diced (US & UK)
- 1 cup corn kernels (fresh, frozen, or canned) (US & UK)
- 2 cups vegetable broth (US & UK)
- 2 tablespoons tomato paste (US & UK)
- 1 tablespoon olive oil (US & UK)
- 1 tablespoon chili powder (US & UK)
- 1 teaspoon ground cumin (US & UK)
- 1/2 teaspoon smoked paprika (US & UK)
- Salt and pepper, to taste
- Fresh cilantro, for garnish (optional)

Instructions:
1. Preheat your air fryer to 375°F (190°C) for 3 minutes. [Function used: Preheat]
2. Heat olive oil in a large skillet over medium heat. Add diced onion, minced garlic, and diced bell pepper. Cook until softened.
3. Stir in chili powder, ground cumin, smoked paprika, salt, and pepper. Cook for another minute until fragrant.
4. Add drained and rinsed black beans, kidney beans, chickpeas, diced tomatoes, corn kernels, vegetable broth, and tomato paste to the skillet. Stir to combine.
5. Bring the chili to a simmer and cook for 1520 minutes, stirring occasionally, until flavors are well blended and chili has thickened slightly.
6. Transfer the vegetarian chili to an air fryersafe baking dish.
7. Place the baking dish in the air fryer basket.
8. Air fry for 1015 minutes until the chili is heated through and bubbling. [Function used: Air frying]
9. Once cooked, garnish the vegetarian chili with fresh cilantro before serving.

Nutritional Info (per serving): Calories: 250 | Fat: 5g | Carbs: 40g | Protein: 12g

Tip: Serve the vegetarian chili with toppings like shredded cheese, diced avocado, sour cream, or tortilla chips.

Baked Falafel with Tzatziki Sauce

Prep: 20 mins | Cook: 20 mins | Serves: 4

Ingredients:

For the Falafel:
- 1 can (15 oz) chickpeas, drained and rinsed (US & UK)
- 1/4 cup fresh parsley, chopped (US & UK)
- 1/4 cup fresh cilantro, chopped (US & UK)
- 1/4 cup diced onion (US & UK) and 2 cloves garlic, minced (US & UK)
- 1 teaspoon ground cumin (US & UK)
- 1 teaspoon ground coriander (US & UK)
- 1/2 teaspoon baking powder (US & UK) & Salt and pepper, to taste
- Olive oil spray (US & UK)

For the Tzatziki Sauce:
- 1/2 cup Greek yogurt (US & UK)
- 1/2 cucumber, grated and squeezed to remove excess moisture (US & UK)
- 1 tablespoon fresh dill, chopped (US & UK) and 1 tablespoon lemon juice (US & UK)
- 1 clove garlic, minced (US & UK) & Salt and pepper, to taste

Instructions:

For the Falafel:
1. Preheat your air fryer to 375°F (190°C) for 3 minutes. [Function used: Preheat]
2. In a food processor, combine chickpeas, chopped parsley, chopped cilantro, diced onion, minced garlic, ground cumin, ground coriander, baking powder, salt, and pepper. Pulse until mixture comes together but still has some texture.
3. Form the chickpea mixture into small balls or patties.
4. Lightly spray the falafel balls or patties with olive oil spray.
5. Place the falafel in the air fryer basket in a single layer.
6. Air fry for 1520 minutes until falafel is crispy and golden brown, shaking the basket halfway through cooking. [Function used: Air frying]

For the Tzatziki Sauce:
1. In a small bowl, mix together Greek yogurt, grated cucumber, lemon juice, chopped dill, minced garlic, salt, and pepper.
2. Stir until well combined.

Assembly:
1. Serve the baked falafel hot with tzatziki sauce for dipping.

Nutritional Info (per serving, including tzatziki sauce): Calories: 200 | Fat: 7g | Carbs: 25g | Protein: 10g

Tip: Serve the baked falafel in pita pockets or over a bed of salad greens for a delicious meal.

CHAPTER 7: BEEF AND PORK

Beef and Vegetable Kebabs

Prep: 20 mins | Cook: 15 mins | Serves: 4

Ingredients:
- 1 lb (450g) beef sirloin or tenderloin, cut into cubes (US & UK)
- 2 bell peppers, cut into chunks (US & UK)
- 1 red onion, cut into chunks (US & UK)
- 8 cherry tomatoes (US & UK)
- 2 tablespoons olive oil (US & UK)
- 2 cloves garlic, minced (US & UK)
- 1 teaspoon dried oregano (US & UK)
- Salt and pepper, to taste
- Wooden skewers, soaked in water

Instructions:
1. Preheat your air fryer to 375°F (190°C) for 3 minutes. [Function used: Preheat]
2. In a bowl, combine beef cubes, bell peppers, red onion, cherry tomatoes, olive oil, minced garlic, dried oregano, salt, and pepper. Toss until well coated.
3. Thread marinated beef and vegetables onto soaked wooden skewers, alternating between ingredients.
4. Place the kebabs in the air fryer basket in a single layer.
5. Air fry for 1215 minutes, turning halfway through, until beef is cooked to your desired level of doneness and vegetables are tender. [Function used: Air frying]
6. Once cooked, remove the kebabs from the air fryer and let them rest for a few minutes before serving.

Nutritional Info (per serving): Calories: 280 | Fat: 14g | Carbs: 10g | Protein: 28g

Tip: Serve the beef and vegetable kebabs with a side of rice or a fresh salad for a complete meal.

Pork Chops with Apple Compote

Prep: 15 mins | Cook: 20 mins | Serves: 4

Ingredients:
- 4 boneless pork chops (about 1 inch thick) (US & UK)
- 2 apples, peeled, cored, and sliced (US & UK)
- 2 tablespoons unsalted butter (US & UK)
- 2 tablespoons brown sugar (US & UK)
- 1 teaspoon ground cinnamon (US & UK)
- 1/4 teaspoon ground nutmeg (US & UK)
- Salt and pepper, to taste

Instructions:
1. Preheat your air fryer to 375°F (190°C) for 3 minutes. [Function used: Preheat]
2. Season pork chops with salt and pepper on both sides.
3. Place pork chops in the air fryer basket in a single layer.
4. Air fry for 1820 minutes, flipping halfway through, until pork chops are cooked through and golden brown. [Function used: Air frying]
5. While the pork chops cook, prepare the apple compote. In a skillet, melt butter over medium heat.
6. Add sliced apples, brown sugar, ground cinnamon, and ground nutmeg to the skillet. Cook, stirring occasionally, until apples are tender and caramelized.
7. Serve the airfried pork chops with a spoonful of apple compote on top.

Nutritional Info (per serving): Calories: 280 | Fat: 14g | Carbs: 18g | Protein: 20g

Tip: Choose firm apples like Granny Smith or Honeycrisp for the compote, as they hold their shape well when cooked.

Meatballs with Marinara Sauce

Prep: 20 mins | Cook: 20 mins | Serves: 4

Ingredients:
- 1 lb (450g) ground beef (US & UK)
- 1/2 cup breadcrumbs (US & UK)
- 1/4 cup grated Parmesan cheese (US & UK)
- 1 egg, beaten (US & UK)
- 2 cloves garlic, minced (US & UK)
- 1 teaspoon dried oregano (US & UK)
- 1/2 teaspoon salt (US & UK)
- 1/4 teaspoon black pepper (US & UK)
- 2 cups marinara sauce (storebought or homemade) (US & UK)

Instructions:
1. In a large bowl, combine ground beef, breadcrumbs, grated Parmesan cheese, beaten egg, minced garlic, dried oregano, salt, and black pepper. Mix until well combined.
2. Shape the mixture into meatballs, about 1 inch in diameter.
3. Preheat your air fryer to 375°F (190°C) for 3 minutes. [Function used: Preheat]
4. Place meatballs in the air fryer basket in a single layer, leaving space between each meatball.
5. Air fry for 1820 minutes, shaking the basket halfway through, until meatballs are cooked through and browned on the outside. [Function used: Air frying]
6. While the meatballs cook, heat marinara sauce in a saucepan over medium heat until warmed through.
7. Serve the airfried meatballs with marinara sauce spooned over the top.

Nutritional Info (per serving, excluding marinara sauce): Calories: 320 | Fat: 20g | Carbs: 8g | Protein: 25g

Tip: You can use ground turkey or chicken instead of beef for a leaner option.

Beef Fajitas

Prep: 15 mins | Cook: 15 mins | Serves: 4

Ingredients:
- 1 lb (450g) beef sirloin or flank steak, thinly sliced (US & UK)
- 1 bell pepper, thinly sliced (US & UK)
- 1 onion, thinly sliced (US & UK)
- 2 tablespoons olive oil (US & UK)
- 1 tablespoon chili powder (US & UK)
- 1 teaspoon ground cumin (US & UK)
- 1 teaspoon smoked paprika (US & UK)
- 1/2 teaspoon garlic powder (US & UK)
- Salt and pepper, to taste
- Flour or corn tortillas, for serving
- Optional toppings: sliced avocado, shredded cheese, sour cream, salsa

Instructions:
1. In a large bowl, combine sliced beef, bell pepper, onion, olive oil, chili powder, ground cumin, smoked paprika, garlic powder, salt, and pepper. Toss until everything is evenly coated.
2. Preheat your air fryer to 375°F (190°C) for 3 minutes. [Function used: Preheat]
3. Place the seasoned beef and vegetable mixture in the air fryer basket in a single layer.
4. Air fry for 1215 minutes, stirring halfway through, until beef is cooked to your desired level of doneness and vegetables are tender. [Function used: Air frying]
5. Warm tortillas in the microwave or on a skillet.
6. Serve the airfried beef and vegetable fajitas with warm tortillas and your choice of toppings.

Nutritional Info (per serving, excluding tortillas and toppings): Calories: 280 | Fat: 15g | Carbs: 10g | Protein: 25g

Tip: For extra flavor, squeeze fresh lime juice over the fajitas before serving.

Pork Tenderloin with Roasted Vegetables

Prep: 15 mins | Cook: 25 mins | Serves: 4

Ingredients:
- 1 lb (450g) pork tenderloin (US & UK)
- 2 cups mixed vegetables (such as carrots, potatoes, Brussels sprouts), diced (US & UK)
- 2 tablespoons olive oil (US & UK)
- 2 cloves garlic, minced (US & UK)
- 1 teaspoon dried thyme (US & UK)
- 1 teaspoon dried rosemary (US & UK)
- Salt and pepper, to taste

Instructions:
1. Preheat your air fryer to 375°F (190°C) for 3 minutes. [Function used: Preheat]
2. In a bowl, toss mixed vegetables with olive oil, minced garlic, dried thyme, dried rosemary, salt, and pepper until well coated.
3. Place the seasoned vegetables in the air fryer basket in a single layer.
4. Air fry for 1215 minutes until vegetables are tender and lightly browned, shaking the basket halfway through. [Function used: Air frying]
5. Season pork tenderloin with salt and pepper on all sides.
6. Place the seasoned pork tenderloin in the air fryer basket alongside the roasted vegetables.
7. Air fry for 2025 minutes, flipping halfway through, until pork is cooked through and internal temperature reaches 145°F (63°C). [Function used: Air frying]
8. Once cooked, let the pork tenderloin rest for a few minutes before slicing.
9. Serve sliced pork tenderloin with roasted vegetables.

Nutritional Info (per serving): Calories: 280 | Fat: 12g | Carbs: 12g | Protein: 30g

Tip: Feel free to customize the roasted vegetables with your favorites, such as broccoli, cauliflower, or bell peppers.

Beef Meatloaf

Prep: 15 mins | Cook: 40 mins | Serves: 4

Ingredients:
- 1 lb (450g) ground beef (US & UK)
- 1/2 cup breadcrumbs (US & UK)
- 1/4 cup grated Parmesan cheese (US & UK)
- 1/4 cup milk (US & UK)
- 1/4 cup ketchup (US & UK)
- 1 egg, beaten (US & UK)
- 1 small onion, finely chopped (US & UK)
- 2 cloves garlic, minced (US & UK)
- 1 teaspoon dried thyme (US & UK)
- 1 teaspoon dried parsley (US & UK)
- 1/2 teaspoon salt (US & UK)
- 1/4 teaspoon black pepper (US & UK)
- Olive oil spray (US & UK)

Instructions:
1. In a large bowl, combine ground beef, breadcrumbs, grated Parmesan cheese, milk, ketchup, beaten egg, chopped onion, minced garlic, dried thyme, dried parsley, salt, and black pepper. Mix until well combined.
2. Preheat your air fryer to 375°F (190°C) for 3 minutes. [Function used: Preheat]
3. Lightly grease the air fryer basket with olive oil spray.
4. Shape the meat mixture into a loaf shape and place it in the greased air fryer basket.
5. Air fry for 35-40 minutes, until the meatloaf is cooked through and reaches an internal temperature of 160°F (71°C). [Function used: Air frying]
6. Once cooked, remove the meatloaf from the air fryer and let it rest for a few minutes before slicing.
7. Serve slices of the beef meatloaf with your favorite sides, such as mashed potatoes and steamed vegetables.

Nutritional Info (per serving): Calories: 350 | Fat: 18g | Carbs: 15g | Protein: 30g

Tip: You can top the meatloaf with additional ketchup or barbecue sauce before air frying for extra flavor.

Pulled Pork Sandwiches

Prep: 15 mins | Cook: 4 hours | Serves: 6

✓ **Ingredients:**
- ✓ 2 lbs (900g) pork shoulder or pork butt, trimmed of excess fat (US & UK)
- ✓ 1 tablespoon brown sugar (US & UK)
- ✓ 1 tablespoon paprika (US & UK)
- ✓ 1 teaspoon garlic powder (US & UK)
- ✓ 1 teaspoon onion powder (US & UK)
- ✓ 1 teaspoon ground cumin (US & UK)
- ✓ 1 teaspoon chili powder (US & UK)
- ✓ Salt and pepper, to taste
- ✓ 1 cup barbecue sauce (storebought or homemade) (US & UK)
- ✓ 6 hamburger buns or sandwich rolls (US & UK)

Instructions:
1. In a small bowl, combine brown sugar, paprika, garlic powder, onion powder, ground cumin, chili powder, salt, and pepper to make a dry rub.
2. Rub the dry rub all over the pork shoulder or pork butt, coating it evenly.
3. Place the seasoned pork in the air fryer basket.
4. Cook at 300°F (150°C) for 4 hours, flipping halfway through, until the pork is tender and easily shreddable. [Function used: Slow cooking]
5. Once the pork is cooked, shred it using two forks.
6. Toss the shredded pork with barbecue sauce until evenly coated.
7. Serve the pulled pork on hamburger buns or sandwich rolls.

Nutritional Info (per serving, excluding buns): Calories: 350 | Fat: 18g | Carbs: 15g | Protein: 30g

Tip: For added flavor, toast the buns before assembling the sandwiches.

Beef Burgers with Caramelized Onions

Prep: 20 mins | Cook: 15 mins | Serves: 4

Ingredients:
- 1 lb (450g) ground beef (US & UK)
- 1 tablespoon Worcestershire sauce (US & UK)
- 1 teaspoon garlic powder (US & UK)
- 1/2 teaspoon onion powder (US & UK)
- Salt and pepper, to taste
- 1 tablespoon olive oil (US & UK)
- 2 onions, thinly sliced (US & UK)
- 4 hamburger buns (US & UK)
- Optional toppings: lettuce, tomato slices, cheese slices

Instructions:
1. In a bowl, combine ground beef, Worcestershire sauce, garlic powder, onion powder, salt, and pepper. Mix until well combined.
2. Divide the beef mixture into 4 equal portions and shape them into burger patties.
3. Preheat your air fryer to 375°F (190°C) for 3 minutes. [Function used: Preheat]
4. Place the burger patties in the air fryer basket in a single layer.
5. Air fry for 1215 minutes, flipping halfway through, until burgers are cooked to your desired level of doneness. [Function used: Air frying]
6. While the burgers cook, heat olive oil in a skillet over mediumlow heat.
7. Add thinly sliced onions to the skillet and cook, stirring occasionally, until caramelized and golden brown, about 1520 minutes.
8. Toast the hamburger buns in the air fryer for 23 minutes until lightly golden.
9. Assemble the beef burgers with caramelized onions and your choice of toppings on toasted buns.

Nutritional Info (per serving, excluding toppings): Calories: 350 | Fat: 18g | Carbs: 25g | Protein: 25g

Tip: You can melt cheese over the burgers during the last minute of air frying for added flavor.

Pork Carnitas

Prep: 15 mins | Cook: 40 mins | Serves: 6

Ingredients:
- 2 lbs (900g) pork shoulder or pork butt, cut into chunks (US & UK)
- 1 tablespoon olive oil (US & UK)
- 1 onion, diced (US & UK)
- 4 cloves garlic, minced (US & UK)
- 1 teaspoon ground cumin (US & UK)
- 1 teaspoon dried oregano (US & UK)
- 1 teaspoon chili powder (US & UK)
- Salt and pepper, to taste
- 1 cup chicken broth (US & UK)
- Juice of 2 limes (US & UK)
- Corn or flour tortillas, for serving
- Optional toppings: chopped cilantro, diced onion, lime wedges

Instructions:
1. Preheat your air fryer to 375°F (190°C) for 3 minutes. [Function used: Preheat]
2. Season pork chunks with salt and pepper.
3. In a large skillet, heat olive oil over medium heat. Add diced onion and minced garlic, and sauté until softened.
4. Add pork chunks to the skillet and brown on all sides.
5. Stir in ground cumin, dried oregano, chili powder, chicken broth, and lime juice. Bring to a simmer.
6. Transfer the pork mixture to the air fryer basket.
7. Air fry for 3540 minutes, stirring occasionally, until pork is tender and starting to brown. [Function used: Air frying]
8. Once cooked, shred the pork using two forks.
9. Serve the pork carnitas with warm tortillas and optional toppings.

Nutritional Info (per serving, excluding tortillas and toppings): Calories: 300 | Fat: 15g | Carbs: 5g | Protein: 35g

Tip: For extra flavor, you can broil the shredded pork in the air fryer for a few minutes after cooking until it gets crispy edges.

Beef Stroganoff

Prep: 15 mins | Cook: 25 mins | Serves: 4

Ingredients:
- 1 lb (450g) beef sirloin or tenderloin, thinly sliced (US & UK)
- 2 tablespoons olive oil (US & UK)
- 1 onion, thinly sliced (US & UK)
- 2 cloves garlic, minced (US & UK)
- 8 oz (225g) mushrooms, sliced (US & UK)
- 2 tablespoons all-purpose flour (US & UK)
- 1 cup beef broth (US & UK)
- 1 tablespoon Worcestershire sauce (US & UK)
- 1/2 cup sour cream (US & UK)
- Salt and pepper, to taste
- Cooked egg noodles or rice, for serving
- Chopped fresh parsley, for garnish (optional)

Instructions:
1. Preheat your air fryer to 375°F (190°C) for 3 minutes. [Function used: Preheat]
2. In a large skillet, heat olive oil over medium heat. Add thinly sliced beef and cook until browned. Remove from skillet and set aside.
3. In the same skillet, add sliced onion, minced garlic, and sliced mushrooms. Sauté until softened.
4. Sprinkle all-purpose flour over the vegetables and cook for 12 minutes, stirring constantly.
5. Gradually stir in beef broth and Worcestershire sauce, scraping up any browned bits from the bottom of the skillet.
6. Return the cooked beef to the skillet and simmer for 1015 minutes until the sauce thickens and beef is cooked through.
7. Meanwhile, cook egg noodles or rice according to package instructions.
8. Stir sour cream into the beef mixture until well combined. Season with salt and pepper to taste.
9. Serve the beef stroganoff over cooked egg noodles or rice, garnished with chopped fresh parsley if desired.

Nutritional Info (per serving, excluding noodles or rice): Calories: 350 | Fat: 20g | Carbs: 10g | Protein: 30g

Tip: For a creamier sauce, you can add more sour cream to taste.

Pork Chops with Mushroom Gravy

Prep: 15 mins | Cook: 20 mins | Serves: 4

Ingredients:
- 4 bonein pork chops (about 1 inch thick) (US & UK)
- Salt and pepper, to taste
- 2 tablespoons olive oil (US & UK)
- 8 oz (225g) mushrooms, sliced (US & UK)
- 1 small onion, diced (US & UK)
- 2 cloves garlic, minced (US & UK)
- 2 tablespoons all-purpose flour (US & UK)
- 1 cup chicken broth (US & UK)
- 1/2 cup heavy cream (US & UK)
- 1 tablespoon Worcestershire sauce (US & UK)
- Fresh chopped parsley, for garnish (optional)

Instructions:
1. Season pork chops with salt and pepper on both sides.
2. Preheat your air fryer to 375°F (190°C) for 3 minutes. [Function used: Preheat]
3. Place pork chops in the air fryer basket in a single layer.
4. Air fry for 1820 minutes, flipping halfway through, until pork chops are cooked through and golden brown. [Function used: Air frying]
5. While the pork chops cook, heat olive oil in a skillet over medium heat. Add sliced mushrooms and diced onion, and cook until softened.
6. Add minced garlic to the skillet and cook for an additional minute.
7. Sprinkle all-purpose flour over the mushrooms and onions, and stir to coat evenly.
8. Gradually pour in chicken broth, stirring constantly until the mixture thickens.
9. Stir in heavy cream and Worcestershire sauce. Simmer for a few minutes until the gravy has reached your desired consistency.
10. Serve the pork chops with mushroom gravy spooned over the top, garnished with fresh chopped parsley if desired.

Nutritional Info (per serving): Calories: 350 | Fat: 25g | Carbs: 8g | Protein: 25g

Tip: For a richer flavor, you can use bonein pork chops.

Salisbury Steak

Prep: 20 mins | Cook: 25 mins | Serves: 4

Ingredients:
- 1 lb (450g) ground beef (US & UK)
- 1/2 cup breadcrumbs (US & UK)
- 1 egg (US & UK)
- 1 small onion, finely chopped (US & UK)
- 2 cloves garlic, minced (US & UK)
- 1 tablespoon Worcestershire sauce (US & UK)
- Salt and pepper, to taste
- 1 tablespoon olive oil (US & UK)
- 8 oz (225g) mushrooms, sliced (US & UK)
- 1 cup beef broth (US & UK)
- 2 tablespoons all-purpose flour (US & UK)
- Chopped fresh parsley, for garnish (optional)

Instructions:
1. In a large bowl, combine ground beef, breadcrumbs, egg, chopped onion, minced garlic, Worcestershire sauce, salt, and pepper. Mix until well combined.
2. Shape the mixture into 4 ovalshaped patties.
3. Preheat your air fryer to 375°F (190°C) for 3 minutes. [Function used: Preheat]
4. Place the beef patties in the air fryer basket in a single layer.
5. Air fry for 1820 minutes, flipping halfway through, until patties are cooked through and browned on the outside. [Function used: Air frying]
6. While the beef patties cook, heat olive oil in a skillet over medium heat. Add sliced mushrooms and cook until softened.
7. In a small bowl, whisk together beef broth and all-purpose flour until smooth.
8. Pour the beef broth mixture into the skillet with the mushrooms. Bring to a simmer and cook until the gravy thickens.
9. Serve the Salisbury steak patties with mushroom gravy spooned over the top, garnished with chopped fresh parsley if desired.

Nutritional Info (per serving): Calories: 350 | Fat: 20g | Carbs: 15g | Protein: 25g

Tip: Serve Salisbury steak with mashed potatoes or steamed vegetables for a complete meal.

Beef Enchiladas

Prep: 20 mins | Cook: 25 mins | Serves: 4

Ingredients:
- 1 lb (450g) ground beef (US & UK)
- 1 small onion, diced (US & UK)
- 2 cloves garlic, minced (US & UK)
- 1 teaspoon ground cumin (US & UK)
- 1 teaspoon chili powder (US & UK)
- Salt and pepper, to taste
- 1 cup enchilada sauce (store-bought or homemade) (US & UK)
- 8 small corn or flour tortillas (US & UK)
- 1 cup shredded cheese (such as cheddar or Monterey Jack) (US & UK)
- Optional toppings: chopped cilantro, diced avocado, sour cream

Instructions:
1. In a skillet, cook ground beef, diced onion, and minced garlic over medium heat until beef is browned and onions are softened.
2. Stir in ground cumin, chili powder, salt, and pepper.
3. Preheat your air fryer to 375°F (190°C) for 3 minutes. [Function used: Preheat]
4. Spoon a portion of the beef mixture onto each tortilla and roll up tightly.
5. Place the rolledup tortillas seam side down in the air fryer basket in a single layer.
6. Pour enchilada sauce over the rolled tortillas, making sure they are evenly coated.
7. Sprinkle shredded cheese over the top of the enchiladas.
8. Air fry for 1215 minutes until the cheese is melted and bubbly, and the enchiladas are heated through. [Function used: Air frying]
9. Once cooked, carefully remove the enchiladas from the air fryer.
10. Serve hot, garnished with optional toppings such as chopped cilantro, diced avocado, and sour cream.

Nutritional Info (per serving): Calories: 400 | Fat: 20g | Carbs: 30g | Protein: 25g

Tip: You can customize the filling by adding beans, corn, or diced peppers for extra flavor and texture.

Pork Chili Verde

Prep: 20 mins | Cook: 30 mins | Serves: 6

Ingredients:
- 1 lb (450g) pork shoulder, trimmed and diced (US & UK)
- Salt and pepper, to taste
- 1 tablespoon olive oil (US & UK)
- 1 onion, diced (US & UK)
- 2 cloves garlic, minced (US & UK)
- 2 cans (4 oz each) diced green chilies (US & UK)
- 2 cans (14 oz each) cannellini beans, drained and rinsed (US & UK)
- 1 can (14 oz) diced tomatoes (US & UK)
- 2 cups chicken broth (US & UK)
- 1 teaspoon ground cumin (US & UK)
- 1 teaspoon dried oregano (US & UK)
- 1/2 teaspoon ground coriander (US & UK)
- Juice of 1 lime (US & UK)
- Chopped fresh cilantro, for garnish (optional)

Instructions:
1. Season diced pork with salt and pepper.
2. Preheat your air fryer to 375°F (190°C) for 3 minutes. [Function used: Preheat]
3. Place seasoned pork in the air fryer basket in a single layer.
4. Air fry for 1520 minutes, stirring occasionally, until pork is browned and cooked through. [Function used: Air frying]
5. While the pork cooks, heat olive oil in a large pot or Dutch oven over medium heat. Add diced onion and minced garlic, and cook until softened.
6. Add diced green chilies, cannellini beans, diced tomatoes, chicken broth, ground cumin, dried oregano, and ground coriander to the pot. Stir to combine.
7. Bring the mixture to a simmer, then reduce heat to low and let it simmer for 1015 minutes, allowing the flavors to meld together.
8. Stir in the cooked pork and lime juice. Simmer for an additional 5 minutes.
9. Serve the pork chili verde hot, garnished with chopped fresh cilantro if desired.

Nutritional Info (per serving): Calories: 300 | Fat: 10g | Carbs: 25g | Protein: 25g

Tip: Serve the chili verde with warm tortillas or rice for a complete meal.

Meatball Subs

Prep: 20 mins | Cook: 20 mins | Serves: 4

Ingredients:
- 1 lb (450g) ground beef (US & UK)
- 1/2 cup breadcrumbs (US & UK)
- 1 egg (US & UK)
- 2 cloves garlic, minced (US & UK)
- 1/4 cup grated Parmesan cheese (US & UK)
- 1 teaspoon dried oregano (US & UK)
- Salt and pepper, to taste
- 4 hoagie rolls or sub rolls (US & UK)
- 1 cup marinara sauce (storebought or homemade) (US & UK)
- 1 cup shredded mozzarella cheese (US & UK)
- Chopped fresh parsley, for garnish (optional)

Instructions:
1. In a large bowl, combine ground beef, breadcrumbs, egg, minced garlic, grated Parmesan cheese, dried oregano, salt, and pepper. Mix until well combined.
2. Preheat your air fryer to 375°F (190°C) for 3 minutes. [Function used: Preheat]
3. Shape the beef mixture into meatballs of equal size.
4. Place the meatballs in the air fryer basket in a single layer.
5. Air fry for 1215 minutes, shaking the basket halfway through, until the meatballs are browned and cooked through. [Function used: Air frying]
6. While the meatballs cook, split the hoagie rolls or sub rolls and lightly toast them in the air fryer for 23 minutes.
7. Heat marinara sauce in a small saucepan over medium heat until warmed through.
8. Place cooked meatballs in the toasted rolls and top with marinara sauce and shredded mozzarella cheese.
9. Return the assembled meatball subs to the air fryer and air fry for an additional 35 minutes, until the cheese is melted and bubbly.
10. Serve the meatball subs hot, garnished with chopped fresh parsley if desired.

Nutritional Info (per serving): Calories: 450 | Fat: 20g | Carbs: 35g | Protein: 30g

Tip: You can customize your meatball subs by adding additional toppings such as sliced peppers, onions, or olives.

CHAPTER 8: SIDE DISHES

Roasted Brussels Sprouts

Prep: 10 mins | Cook: 15 mins | Serves: 4

Ingredients:
- 1 lb (450g) Brussels sprouts, trimmed and halved (US & UK)
- 2 tablespoons olive oil (US & UK) and Salt and pepper, to taste
- Optional: balsamic glaze for drizzling

Instructions:
1. Preheat your air fryer to 375°F (190°C) for 3 minutes. [Function used: Preheat]
2. In a bowl, toss Brussels sprouts with olive oil, salt, and pepper until evenly coated.
3. Place the Brussels sprouts in the air fryer basket in a single layer.
4. Air fry for 1215 minutes, shaking the basket halfway through, until Brussels sprouts are crispy and tender. [Function used: Air frying]
5. Once cooked, transfer to a serving dish and drizzle with balsamic glaze if desired.
6. Serve hot as a delicious and nutritious side dish.

Nutritional Info (per serving): Calories: 100 | Fat: 7g | Carbs: 9g | Protein: 4g

Mashed Cauliflower

Prep: 10 mins | Cook: 15 mins | Serves: 4

Ingredients:
- 1 head cauliflower, cut into florets (US & UK)
- 2 cloves garlic, minced (US & UK) and Salt and pepper, to taste
- 2 tablespoons unsalted butter (US & UK)
- Optional: chopped chives for garnish

Instructions:
1. Place cauliflower florets in a microwavesafe bowl with minced garlic and a splash of water.
2. Microwave on high for 810 minutes until cauliflower is tender.
3. Drain excess water and transfer cauliflower to a food processor or blender.
4. Add unsalted butter, salt, and pepper to the cauliflower.
5. Blend until smooth and creamy, scraping down the sides as needed.
6. Preheat your air fryer to 375°F (190°C) for 3 minutes. [Function used: Preheat]
7. Transfer mashed cauliflower to an ovensafe dish and place it in the air fryer basket.
8. Air fry for 1015 minutes until the top is lightly golden and heated through. [Function used: Air frying]
9. Garnish with chopped chives if desired and serve hot.

Nutritional Info (per serving): Calories: 80 | Fat: 5g | Carbs: 8g | Protein: 3g

AirFried Asparagus

Prep: 5 mins | Cook: 10 mins | Serves: 4

Ingredients:
- ✓ 1 lb (450g) asparagus spears, trimmed (US & UK)
- ✓ 1 tablespoon olive oil (US & UK)
- ✓ Salt and pepper, to taste
- ✓ Grated Parmesan cheese (optional)

Instructions:
1. Preheat your air fryer to 400°F (200°C) for 3 minutes. [Function used: Preheat]
2. Place asparagus spears in a bowl and drizzle with olive oil. Toss to coat evenly.
3. Season with salt and pepper.
4. Arrange the asparagus in the air fryer basket in a single layer.
5. Air fry for 810 minutes until the asparagus is tender and slightly crispy. [Function used: Air frying]
6. Once cooked, remove from the air fryer and sprinkle with grated Parmesan cheese if desired.
7. Serve hot as a tasty side dish.

Nutritional Info (per serving): Calories: 40 | Fat: 3g | Carbs: 4g | Protein: 2g

Roasted Sweet Potato Wedges

Prep: 10 mins | Cook: 20 mins | Serves: 4

Ingredients:
- ✓ 2 large sweet potatoes, scrubbed and cut into wedges (US & UK)
- ✓ 2 tablespoons olive oil (US & UK)
- ✓ 1 teaspoon paprika (US & UK)
- ✓ 1/2 teaspoon garlic powder (US & UK) and Salt and pepper, to taste
- ✓ Fresh parsley, chopped (optional)

Instructions:
1. Preheat your air fryer to 400°F (200°C) for 3 minutes. [Function used: Preheat]
2. In a bowl, toss sweet potato wedges with olive oil, paprika, garlic powder, salt, and pepper until evenly coated.
3. Place the sweet potato wedges in the air fryer basket in a single layer.
4. Air fry for 1820 minutes, shaking the basket halfway through, until the sweet potatoes are tender and crispy. [Function used: Air frying]
5. Once cooked, transfer to a serving dish and sprinkle with fresh chopped parsley if desired.
6. Serve hot as a nutritious and flavorful side dish.

Nutritional Info (per serving): Calories: 150 | Fat: 7g | Carbs: 21g | Protein: 2g

Garlic Parmesan Zucchini Noodles

Prep: 10 mins | Cook: 10 mins | Serves: 4

Ingredients:
- ✓ 4 medium zucchinis, spiralized into noodles (US & UK)
- ✓ 2 tablespoons olive oil (US & UK)
- ✓ 2 cloves garlic, minced (US & UK)
- ✓ 1/4 cup grated Parmesan cheese (US & UK)
- ✓ Salt and pepper, to taste
- ✓ Fresh chopped parsley, for garnish (optional)

Instructions:
1. Preheat your air fryer to 375°F (190°C) for 3 minutes. [Function used: Preheat]
2. In a bowl, toss zucchini noodles with olive oil and minced garlic until evenly coated.
3. Season with salt and pepper.
4. Place the zucchini noodles in the air fryer basket in a single layer.
5. Air fry for 810 minutes until the zucchini noodles are tender and slightly golden. [Function used: Air frying]
6. Once cooked, transfer to a serving dish and sprinkle with grated Parmesan cheese.
7. Garnish with fresh chopped parsley if desired.
8. Serve hot as a flavorful and lowcarb side dish.

Nutritional Info (per serving): Calories: 90 | Fat: 7g | Carbs: 5g | Protein: 3g

Roasted Beets

Prep: 10 mins | Cook: 30 mins | Serves: 4

Ingredients:
- ✓ 4 medium beets, peeled and diced (US & UK)
- ✓ 2 tablespoons olive oil (US & UK) and Salt and pepper, to taste
- ✓ Fresh thyme leaves, for garnish (optional)

Instructions:
1. Preheat your air fryer to 375°F (190°C) for 3 minutes. [Function used: Preheat]
2. In a bowl, toss diced beets with olive oil, salt, and pepper until evenly coated.
3. Place the seasoned beets in the air fryer basket in a single layer.
4. Air fry for 2530 minutes, shaking the basket halfway through, until the beets are tender and caramelized. [Function used: Air frying]
5. Once cooked, transfer to a serving dish and garnish with fresh thyme leaves if desired.
6. Serve hot as a vibrant and nutritious side dish.

Nutritional Info (per serving): Calories: 80 | Fat: 5g | Carbs: 9g | Protein: 1g

Crispy Roasted Potatoes

Prep: 10 mins | Cook: 25 mins | Serves: 4

Ingredients:
- 1 lb (450g) baby potatoes, halved (US & UK)
- 2 tablespoons olive oil (US & UK)
- 1 teaspoon garlic powder (US & UK)
- 1 teaspoon dried thyme (US & UK)
- Salt and pepper, to taste
- Fresh chopped parsley, for garnish (optional)

Instructions:
1. Preheat your air fryer to 400°F (200°C) for 3 minutes. [Function used: Preheat]
2. In a bowl, toss halved baby potatoes with olive oil, garlic powder, dried thyme, salt, and pepper until evenly coated.
3. Place the seasoned potatoes in the air fryer basket in a single layer.
4. Air fry for 2025 minutes, shaking the basket halfway through, until the potatoes are crispy and golden brown. [Function used: Air frying]
5. Once cooked, transfer to a serving dish and sprinkle with fresh chopped parsley if desired.
6. Serve hot as a delicious and satisfying side dish.

Nutritional Info (per serving): Calories: 150 | Fat: 7g | Carbs: 20g | Protein: 2g

AirFried Green Beans

Prep: 5 mins | Cook: 10 mins | Serves: 4

Ingredients:
- 1 lb (450g) fresh green beans, trimmed (US & UK)
- 1 tablespoon olive oil (US & UK)
- 1/2 teaspoon garlic powder (US & UK)
- 1/2 teaspoon smoked paprika (US & UK) and Salt and pepper, to taste
- Grated Parmesan cheese, for topping (optional)

Instructions:
1. Preheat your air fryer to 375°F (190°C) for 3 minutes. [Function used: Preheat]
2. In a bowl, toss trimmed green beans with olive oil, garlic powder, smoked paprika, salt, and pepper until evenly coated.
3. Place the seasoned green beans in the air fryer basket in a single layer.
4. Air fry for 810 minutes until the green beans are tender and slightly crispy. [Function used: Air frying]
5. Once cooked, transfer to a serving dish and sprinkle with grated Parmesan cheese if desired.
6. Serve hot as a nutritious and flavorful side dish.

Nutritional Info (per serving): Calories: 60 | Fat: 3g | Carbs: 8g | Protein: 2g

Cauliflower Rice Pilaf

Prep: 10 mins | Cook: 10 mins | Serves: 4

Ingredients:
- 1 head cauliflower, grated into ricelike pieces (US & UK)
- 2 tablespoons olive oil (US & UK) and 1 onion, diced (US & UK)
- 2 cloves garlic, minced (US & UK)
- 1/4 cup chopped parsley (US & UK)
- Salt and pepper, to taste

Instructions:
1. Preheat your air fryer to 375°F (190°C) for 3 minutes. [Function used: Preheat]
2. In a bowl, toss grated cauliflower with olive oil, diced onion, minced garlic, chopped parsley, salt, and pepper until well combined.
3. Place the seasoned cauliflower mixture in the air fryer basket.
4. Air fry for 8-10 minutes, stirring halfway through, until the cauliflower is tender and lightly browned. [Function used: Air frying]
5. Once cooked, transfer to a serving dish and serve hot as a healthy and flavorful side dish.

Nutritional Info (per serving): Calories: 70 | Fat: 5g | Carbs: 6g | Protein: 2g

Broccoli and Cheddar Fritters

Prep: 15 mins | Cook: 15 mins | Serves: 4

Ingredients:
- 2 cups broccoli florets, steamed and chopped (US & UK)
- 1 cup grated cheddar cheese (US & UK)
- 1/4 cup breadcrumbs (US & UK) and 2 eggs, beaten (US & UK)
- 2 tablespoons chopped green onions (US & UK)
- Salt and pepper, to taste and Cooking spray

Instructions:
1. In a large bowl, combine chopped broccoli florets, grated cheddar cheese, breadcrumbs, beaten eggs, chopped green onions, salt, and pepper. Mix until well combined.
2. Preheat your air fryer to 375°F (190°C) for 3 minutes. [Function used: Preheat]
3. Shape the broccoli mixture into small fritters.
4. Lightly coat the air fryer basket with cooking spray.
5. Place the fritters in the air fryer basket in a single layer, leaving space between each fritter.
6. Air fry for 12-15 minutes, flipping halfway through, until the fritters are golden and crispy. [Function used: Air frying]
7. Once cooked, transfer the fritters to a serving dish and serve hot as a tasty side dish or snack.

Nutritional Info (per serving): Calories: 180 | Fat: 10g | Carbs: 11g | Protein: 10g

Roasted Butternut Squash
Prep: 15 mins | Cook: 25 mins | Serves: 4

Ingredients:
- 1 butternut squash, peeled, seeded, and diced (US & UK)
- 2 tablespoons olive oil (US & UK) and 1 tablespoon maple syrup (US & UK)
- 1 teaspoon ground cinnamon (US & UK) and Salt and pepper, to taste
- Chopped fresh parsley, for garnish (optional)

Instructions:
1. Preheat your air fryer to 375°F (190°C) for 3 minutes. [Function used: Preheat]
2. In a bowl, toss diced butternut squash with olive oil, maple syrup, ground cinnamon, salt, and pepper until evenly coated.
3. Place the seasoned butternut squash in the air fryer basket in a single layer.
4. Air fry for 2025 minutes, shaking the basket halfway through, until the squash is tender and caramelized. [Function used: Air frying]
5. Once cooked, transfer to a serving dish and garnish with chopped fresh parsley if desired.
6. Serve hot as a delicious and nutritious side dish.

Nutritional Info (per serving): Calories: 120 | Fat: 7g | Carbs: 15g | Protein: 1g

AirFried Eggplant with Marinara

Prep: 15 mins | Cook: 20 mins | Serves: 4

Ingredients:
- 1 large eggplant, sliced into rounds (US & UK)
- 1 cup marinara sauce (US & UK) and 1/2 cup grated mozzarella cheese (US & UK)
- 1/4 cup grated Parmesan cheese (US & UK) and Salt and pepper, to taste
- 1 teaspoon Italian seasoning (US & UK) and Fresh basil leaves, for garnish (optional)

Instructions:
1. Preheat your air fryer to 375°F (190°C) for 3 minutes. [Function used: Preheat]
2. Season eggplant slices with salt and let them sit for 10 minutes to release excess moisture. Pat dry with paper towels.
3. Brush both sides of the eggplant slices with olive oil.
4. Place the eggplant slices in the air fryer basket in a single layer.
5. Air fry for 10 minutes, flipping halfway through, until the eggplant is golden and tender.
6. Top each eggplant slice with marinara sauce, grated mozzarella cheese, and grated Parmesan cheese.
7. Sprinkle with Italian seasoning, salt, and pepper.
8. Air fry for an additional 57 minutes until the cheese is melted and bubbly.
9. Once cooked, garnish with fresh basil leaves if desired.
10. Serve hot as a delicious and satisfying side dish or appetizer.

Nutritional Info (per serving): Calories: 150 | Fat: 9g | Carbs: 11g | Protein: 7g

Loaded Mashed Cauliflower

Prep: 10 mins | Cook: 20 mins | Serves: 4

Ingredients:
- 1 head cauliflower, cut into florets (US & UK)
- 2 cloves garlic, minced (US & UK)
- 2 tablespoons unsalted butter (US & UK)
- 1/4 cup shredded cheddar cheese (US & UK)
- 2 tablespoons chopped green onions (US & UK)
- Salt and pepper, to taste

Instructions:
1. Place cauliflower florets in a microwavesafe bowl with minced garlic and a splash of water.
2. Microwave on high for 810 minutes until cauliflower is tender.
3. Drain excess water and transfer cauliflower to a food processor or blender.
4. Add unsalted butter, shredded cheddar cheese, chopped green onions, salt, and pepper to the cauliflower.
5. Blend until smooth and creamy, scraping down the sides as needed.
6. Preheat your air fryer to 375°F (190°C) for 3 minutes. [Function used: Preheat]
7. Transfer mashed cauliflower to an ovensafe dish and place it in the air fryer basket.
8. Air fry for 1015 minutes until the top is lightly golden and heated through. [Function used: Air frying]
9. Once cooked, serve hot as a flavorful and lowcarb side dish.

Nutritional Info (per serving): Calories: 120 | Fat: 8g | Carbs: 9g | Protein: 4g

Roasted Carrots with HoneyMustard Glaze

Prep: 10 mins | Cook: 20 mins | Serves: 4

Ingredients:
- 1 lb (450g) baby carrots (US & UK)
- 2 tablespoons olive oil (US & UK)
- 2 tablespoons honey (US & UK)
- 1 tablespoon Dijon mustard (US & UK)
- Salt and pepper, to taste
- Fresh parsley, chopped, for garnish (optional)

Instructions:
1. Preheat your air fryer to 375°F (190°C) for 3 minutes. [Function used: Preheat]
2. In a bowl, toss baby carrots with olive oil, honey, Dijon mustard, salt, and pepper until evenly coated.
3. Place the seasoned carrots in the air fryer basket in a single layer.
4. Air fry for 1820 minutes, shaking the basket halfway through, until the carrots are tender and caramelized. [Function used: Air frying]
5. Once cooked, transfer to a serving dish and sprinkle with chopped fresh parsley if desired.
6. Serve hot as a sweet and savory side dish.

Nutritional Info (per serving): Calories: 100 | Fat: 5g | Carbs: 15g | Protein: 1g

Zucchini Fritters

Prep: 15 mins | Cook: 15 mins | Serves: 4

Ingredients:
- 2 medium zucchinis, grated and squeezed dry (US & UK)
- 1/4 cup all-purpose flour (US & UK)
- 1/4 cup grated Parmesan cheese (US & UK)
- 2 cloves garlic, minced (US & UK)
- 1 egg, beaten (US & UK)
- 2 tablespoons chopped fresh parsley (US & UK)
- Salt and pepper, to taste
- Cooking spray

Instructions:
1. In a large bowl, combine grated zucchini, all-purpose flour, grated Parmesan cheese, minced garlic, beaten egg, chopped fresh parsley, salt, and pepper. Mix until well combined.
2. Preheat your air fryer to 375°F (190°C) for 3 minutes. [Function used: Preheat]
3. Lightly coat the air fryer basket with cooking spray.
4. Scoop spoonfuls of the zucchini mixture and shape them into fritters.
5. Place the fritters in the air fryer basket in a single layer, leaving space between each fritter.
6. Air fry for 1215 minutes, flipping halfway through, until the fritters are golden and crispy. [Function used: Air frying]
7. Once cooked, transfer the fritters to a serving dish and serve hot as a delicious and nutritious side dish or snack.

Nutritional Info (per serving): Calories: 90 | Fat: 3g | Carbs: 12g | Protein: 4g

CHAPTER 9: BREADS AND BAKED GOODS

Whole Wheat Dinner Rolls

Prep: 15 mins | Cook: 15 mins | Serves: 12 rolls

Ingredients:
- 2 cups whole-wheat flour (US & UK)
- 1 cup all-purpose flour (US & UK)
- 1 packet (2 1/4 tsp) active dry yeast (US & UK)
- 1 cup warm water (110°F/45°C) (US & UK)
- 2 tablespoons honey (US & UK)
- 2 tablespoons olive oil (US & UK)
- 1 teaspoon salt (US & UK)
- Cooking spray

Instructions:
1. In a bowl, dissolve yeast in warm water and let it sit for 5 minutes until foamy.
2. Add honey, olive oil, and salt to the yeast mixture.
3. Gradually add wholewheat flour and all-purpose flour, stirring until a dough forms.
4. Knead the dough on a floured surface for 57 minutes until smooth and elastic.
5. Place the dough in a greased bowl, cover with a clean towel, and let it rise in a warm place for 1 hour or until doubled in size.
6. Preheat your air fryer to 375°F (190°C) for 3 minutes. [Function used: Preheat]
7. Punch down the risen dough and divide it into 12 equal portions.
8. Shape each portion into a roll and place them in the air fryer basket, leaving space between each roll.
9. Air fry for 1215 minutes until the rolls are golden brown and sound hollow when tapped on the bottom. [Function used: Air frying]
10. Once cooked, transfer the rolls to a wire rack to cool slightly before serving.

Nutritional Info (per serving): Calories: 120 | Fat: 3g | Carbs: 20g | Protein: 4g

AirFried Bagels

Prep: 20 mins | Cook: 15 mins | Serves: 6 bagels

Ingredients:
- ✓ 1 1/2 cups all-purpose flour (US & UK)
- ✓ 1 teaspoon instant yeast (US & UK)
- ✓ 1 tablespoon honey (US & UK)
- ✓ 1/2 teaspoon salt (US & UK)
- ✓ 3/4 cup warm water (110°F/45°C) (US & UK)
- ✓ 1 egg, beaten (for egg wash) (US & UK)
- ✓ Optional toppings: sesame seeds, poppy seeds, dried onion flakes

Instructions:
1. In a large bowl, combine flour, instant yeast, honey, and salt.
2. Gradually add warm water, stirring until a dough forms.
3. Knead the dough on a floured surface for 57 minutes until smooth and elastic.
4. Divide the dough into 6 equal portions and shape each portion into a bagel.
5. Preheat your air fryer to 375°F (190°C) for 3 minutes. [Function used: Preheat]
6. Place the bagels in the air fryer basket, leaving space between each bagel.
7. Brush the tops of the bagels with beaten egg and sprinkle with desired toppings.
8. Air fry for 1215 minutes until the bagels are golden brown and cooked through. [Function used: Air frying]
9. Once cooked, transfer the bagels to a wire rack to cool before serving.

Nutritional Info (per serving): Calories: 180 | Fat: 1g | Carbs: 35g | Protein: 6g

Zucchini Bread

Prep: 15 mins | Cook: 35 mins | Serves: 10 slices

Ingredients:
- 2 cups grated zucchini (US & UK)
- 1 1/2 cups all-purpose flour (US & UK)
- 1/2 cup wholewheat flour (US & UK)
- 1 teaspoon baking powder (US & UK)
- 1/2 teaspoon baking soda (US & UK)
- 1 teaspoon ground cinnamon (US & UK)
- 1/2 teaspoon salt (US & UK)
- 2 eggs (US & UK)
- 1/2 cup unsweetened applesauce (US & UK)
- 1/4 cup honey (US & UK)
- 1/4 cup olive oil (US & UK)
- 1 teaspoon vanilla extract (US & UK)

Instructions:
1. Preheat your air fryer to 325°F (160°C) for 3 minutes. [Function used: Preheat]
2. In a large bowl, combine grated zucchini, all-purpose flour, wholewheat flour, baking powder, baking soda, cinnamon, and salt.
3. In another bowl, whisk together eggs, applesauce, honey, olive oil, and vanilla extract.
4. Pour the wet ingredients into the dry ingredients and stir until just combined.
5. Pour the batter into a greased loaf pan that fits in your air fryer basket.
6. Place the loaf pan in the air fryer basket and air fry for 3035 minutes until a toothpick inserted into the center comes out clean. [Function used: Air frying]
7. Once cooked, remove the zucchini bread from the air fryer and let it cool in the pan for 10 minutes before transferring it to a wire rack to cool completely.

Nutritional Info (per serving): Calories: 180 | Fat: 6g | Carbs: 28g | Protein: 4g

Banana Bread

Prep: 15 mins | Cook: 35 mins | Serves: 10 slices

Ingredients:
- 3 ripe bananas, mashed (US & UK)
- 1/3 cup melted coconut oil (US & UK)
- 1/2 cup honey (US & UK)
- 2 eggs (US & UK)
- 1 teaspoon vanilla extract (US & UK)
- 1 3/4 cups wholewheat flour (US & UK)
- 1 teaspoon baking soda (US & UK)
- 1/2 teaspoon salt (US & UK)
- Optional addins: chopped nuts, chocolate chips

Instructions:
1. Preheat your air fryer to 325°F (160°C) for 3 minutes. [Function used: Preheat]
2. In a large bowl, mix mashed bananas, melted coconut oil, honey, eggs, and vanilla extract.
3. Add wholewheat flour, baking soda, and salt to the wet ingredients and stir until just combined.
4. If using, fold in chopped nuts or chocolate chips.
5. Pour the batter into a greased loaf pan that fits in your air fryer basket.
6. Place the loaf pan in the air fryer basket and air fry for 3035 minutes until a toothpick inserted into the center comes out clean. [Function used: Air frying]
7. Once cooked, remove the banana bread from the air fryer and let it cool in the pan for 10 minutes before transferring it to a wire rack to cool completely.

Nutritional Info (per serving): Calories: 220 | Fat: 8g | Carbs: 35g | Protein: 4g

Pumpkin Bread

Prep: 15 mins | Cook: 35 mins | Serves: 10 slices

Ingredients:
- 1 3/4 cups wholewheat flour (US & UK)
- 1 teaspoon baking soda (US & UK)
- 1/2 teaspoon baking powder (US & UK)
- 1 teaspoon ground cinnamon (US & UK)
- 1/2 teaspoon ground nutmeg (US & UK)
- 1/4 teaspoon ground cloves (US & UK)
- 1/2 teaspoon salt (US & UK)
- 1 cup pumpkin puree (US & UK)
- 1/2 cup honey (US & UK)
- 1/3 cup melted coconut oil (US & UK)
- 2 eggs (US & UK)
- 1 teaspoon vanilla extract (US & UK)

Instructions:
1. Preheat your air fryer to 325°F (160°C) for 3 minutes. [Function used: Preheat]
2. In a large bowl, whisk together wholewheat flour, baking soda, baking powder, cinnamon, nutmeg, cloves, and salt.
3. In another bowl, mix pumpkin puree, honey, melted coconut oil, eggs, and vanilla extract until well combined.
4. Pour the wet ingredients into the dry ingredients and stir until just combined.
5. Pour the batter into a greased loaf pan that fits in your air fryer basket.
6. Place the loaf pan in the air fryer basket and air fry for 3035 minutes until a toothpick inserted into the center comes out clean. [Function used: Air frying]
7. Once cooked, remove the pumpkin bread from the air fryer and let it cool in the pan for 10 minutes before transferring it to a wire rack to cool completely.

Nutritional Info (per serving): Calories: 200 | Fat: 9g | Carbs: 28g | Protein: 4g

WholeWheat Pizza Crust

Prep: 15 mins | Cook: 10 mins | Serves: 4

Ingredients:
- ✓ 1 cup wholewheat flour (US & UK)
- ✓ 1 cup all-purpose flour (US & UK)
- ✓ 1 packet (2 1/4 tsp) instant yeast (US & UK)
- ✓ 1 teaspoon salt (US & UK)
- ✓ 1 tablespoon honey (US & UK)
- ✓ 1 tablespoon olive oil (US & UK)
- ✓ 3/4 cup warm water (110°F/45°C) (US & UK)
- ✓ Cooking spray

Instructions:
1. In a large bowl, combine wholewheat flour, all-purpose flour, instant yeast, and salt.
2. Add honey, olive oil, and warm water to the flour mixture. Stir until a dough forms.
3. Knead the dough on a floured surface for 57 minutes until smooth and elastic.
4. Place the dough in a greased bowl, cover with a clean towel, and let it rise in a warm place for 1 hour or until doubled in size.
5. Preheat your air fryer to 400°F (200°C) for 3 minutes. [Function used: Preheat]
6. Punch down the risen dough and divide it into 4 equal portions.
7. Roll out each portion of dough into a circle or desired shape.
8. Lightly coat the air fryer basket with cooking spray.
9. Place the pizza dough in the air fryer basket, one at a time, making sure not to overlap.
10. Air fry for 5 minutes until the crust is lightly golden and firm. [Function used: Air frying]
11. Once cooked, remove the pizza crust from the air fryer and add desired toppings.
12. Return the pizza to the air fryer and air fry for an additional 5 minutes until the toppings are heated through and the crust is crisp.
13. Once cooked to your liking, remove the pizza from the air fryer, slice, and serve hot.

Nutritional Info (per serving): Calories: 220 | Fat: 3g | Carbs: 42g | Protein: 7g

AirFried Biscuits

Prep: 10 mins | Cook: 10 mins | Serves: 6 biscuits

Ingredients:
- 2 cups all-purpose flour (US & UK)
- 1 tablespoon baking powder (US & UK)
- 1 teaspoon salt (US & UK)
- 1/4 cup unsalted butter, cold and cubed (US & UK)
- 3/4 cup milk (US & UK)
- Cooking spray

Instructions:
1. In a large bowl, whisk together all-purpose flour, baking powder, and salt.
2. Add cold cubed butter to the flour mixture and cut it in using a pastry cutter or fork until it resembles coarse crumbs.
3. Gradually add milk to the mixture, stirring until a dough forms.
4. Turn the dough out onto a floured surface and knead gently for 12 minutes.
5. Roll out the dough to about 1/2inch thickness.
6. Preheat your air fryer to 350°F (180°C) for 3 minutes. [Function used: Preheat]
7. Lightly coat the air fryer basket with cooking spray.
8. Use a biscuit cutter to cut out biscuits from the dough and place them in the air fryer basket, leaving space between each biscuit.
9. Air fry for 810 minutes until the biscuits are golden brown and cooked through. [Function used: Air frying]
10. Once cooked, remove the biscuits from the air fryer and serve warm.

Nutritional Info (per serving): Calories: 230 | Fat: 8g | Carbs: 34g | Protein: 5g

Cornbread

Prep: 10 mins | Cook: 20 mins | Serves: 8 slices

Ingredients:
- 1 cup cornmeal (US & UK)
- 1 cup all-purpose flour (US & UK)
- 1 tablespoon baking powder (US & UK)
- 1/2 teaspoon salt (US & UK)
- 1 cup milk (US & UK)
- 1/4 cup unsalted butter, melted (US & UK)
- 1/4 cup honey (US & UK)
- 2 eggs (US & UK)

Instructions:
1. In a large bowl, whisk together cornmeal, all-purpose flour, baking powder, and salt.
2. In another bowl, whisk together milk, melted butter, honey, and eggs until well combined.
3. Pour the wet ingredients into the dry ingredients and stir until just combined.
4. Preheat your air fryer to 375°F (190°C) for 3 minutes. [Function used: Preheat]
5. Lightly grease a baking pan that fits in your air fryer basket.
6. Pour the cornbread batter into the prepared baking pan.
7. Place the pan in the air fryer basket and air fry for 1820 minutes until the cornbread is golden brown and a toothpick inserted into the center comes out clean. [Function used: Air frying]
8. Once cooked, remove the cornbread from the air fryer and let it cool slightly before slicing and serving.

Nutritional Info (per serving): Calories: 240 | Fat: 9g | Carbs: 35g | Protein: 5g

AirFried Donuts

Prep: 15 mins | Cook: 10 mins | Serves: 6 donuts

Ingredients:
- 1 can (16 oz) refrigerated biscuit dough (US & UK)
- 1/4 cup granulated sugar (US & UK)
- 1 tablespoon ground cinnamon (US & UK)
- 2 tablespoons unsalted butter, melted (US & UK)

Instructions:
1. Remove the biscuits from the can and separate them.
2. Use a small biscuit cutter or bottle cap to cut out the centers of each biscuit to form donuts.
3. Preheat your air fryer to 350°F (180°C) for 3 minutes. [Function used: Preheat]
4. Lightly coat the air fryer basket with cooking spray.
5. Place the donuts in the air fryer basket, leaving space between each donut.
6. Air fry for 5 minutes.
7. Meanwhile, mix granulated sugar and ground cinnamon in a shallow bowl.
8. Remove the donuts from the air fryer and brush them with melted butter.
9. Coat the donuts in the cinnamon sugar mixture until fully coated.
10. Return the coated donuts to the air fryer and air fry for an additional 35 minutes until golden brown and cooked through. [Function used: Air frying]
11. Once cooked, remove the donuts from the air fryer and let them cool slightly before serving.

Nutritional Info (per serving): Calories: 210 | Fat: 8g | Carbs: 30g | Protein: 3g

WholeWheat Tortillas

Prep: 10 mins | Cook: 5 mins | Serves: 6 tortillas

Ingredients:
- ✓ 1 cup wholewheat flour (US & UK)
- ✓ 1/2 teaspoon salt (US & UK)
- ✓ 1 tablespoon olive oil (US & UK)
- ✓ 1/2 cup warm water (US & UK)

Instructions:
1. In a bowl, mix wholewheat flour and salt.
2. Add olive oil and warm water to the flour mixture.
3. Stir until the dough comes together, then knead for a few minutes until smooth.
4. Divide the dough into 6 equal portions and roll each portion into a ball.
5. Preheat your air fryer to 375°F (190°C) for 3 minutes. [Function used: Preheat]
6. On a floured surface, roll out each dough ball into a thin circle.
7. Place a tortilla in the air fryer basket and cook for 23 minutes on each side until lightly browned and cooked through. [Function used: Air frying]
8. Repeat with the remaining dough balls.
9. Once cooked, stack the tortillas on a plate and cover with a clean towel to keep warm until ready to serve.

Nutritional Info (per serving): Calories: 100 | Fat: 3g | Carbs: 15g | Protein: 3g

Garlic Knots

Prep: 15 mins | Cook: 10 mins | Serves: 4

Ingredients:
- 1 pound pizza dough (US & UK)
- 2 tablespoons unsalted butter, melted (US & UK)
- 2 cloves garlic, minced (US & UK)
- 1 tablespoon chopped fresh parsley (US & UK)
- 1/4 teaspoon salt (US & UK)
- Cooking spray

Instructions:
1. Preheat your air fryer to 375°F (190°C) for 3 minutes. [Function used: Preheat]
2. Divide the pizza dough into 12 equal portions.
3. Roll each portion into a rope, about 6 inches long.
4. Tie each rope into a knot and tuck the ends underneath.
5. Place the knots in the air fryer basket, making sure they're not touching.
6. Lightly coat the knots with cooking spray.
7. Air fry for 810 minutes until golden brown and cooked through. [Function used: Air frying]
8. In a small bowl, mix melted butter, minced garlic, chopped parsley, and salt.
9. Once the knots are done, remove them from the air fryer and brush them with the garlic butter mixture.
10. Serve the garlic knots warm.

Nutritional Info (per serving): Calories: 220 | Fat: 8g | Carbs: 32g | Protein: 5g

Prep: 20 mins | Cook: 12 mins | Serves: 6 rolls

Ingredients:
- 1 pound pizza dough (US & UK)
- 3 tablespoons unsalted butter, melted (US & UK)
- 1/4 cup granulated sugar (US & UK)
- 1 tablespoon ground cinnamon (US & UK)
- 1/4 cup powdered sugar (US & UK)
- 1 tablespoon milk (US & UK)
- 1/4 teaspoon vanilla extract (US & UK)

Instructions:
1. Preheat your air fryer to 375°F (190°C) for 3 minutes. [Function used: Preheat]
2. Roll out the pizza dough into a rectangle, about 1/4 inch thick.
3. Brush the melted butter over the dough.
4. In a small bowl, mix granulated sugar and ground cinnamon. Sprinkle this mixture evenly over the buttered dough.
5. Starting from one long edge, tightly roll up the dough into a log.
6. Cut the log into 6 equal pieces.
7. Place the cinnamon rolls in the air fryer basket, cut side up, leaving space between each roll.
8. Air fry for 1012 minutes until the rolls are golden brown and cooked through. [Function used: Air frying]
9. In another small bowl, whisk together powdered sugar, milk, and vanilla extract to make the glaze.
10. Once the cinnamon rolls are done, drizzle them with the glaze.
11. Serve the cinnamon rolls warm.

Nutritional Info (per serving): Calories: 280 | Fat: 9g | Carbs: 46g | Protein: 5g

WholeWheat Waffles

Prep: 10 mins | Cook: 10 mins | Serves: 4 waffles

Ingredients:
- 1 cup wholewheat flour (US & UK)
- 1 tablespoon baking powder (US & UK)
- 1/4 teaspoon salt (US & UK)
- 1 tablespoon granulated sugar (US & UK)
- 1 egg (US & UK)
- 1 cup milk (US & UK)
- 2 tablespoons unsalted butter, melted (US & UK)
- Cooking spray

Instructions:
1. In a large bowl, whisk together wholewheat flour, baking powder, salt, and granulated sugar.
2. In another bowl, whisk together egg, milk, and melted butter.
3. Pour the wet ingredients into the dry ingredients and stir until just combined.
4. Preheat your waffle iron according to manufacturer's instructions.
5. Lightly coat the waffle iron with cooking spray.
6. Pour enough batter onto the center of the waffle iron to cover the grids.
7. Close the waffle iron and cook according to manufacturer's instructions until the waffles are golden brown and crisp.
8. Once done, remove the waffles from the waffle iron and repeat with the remaining batter.
9. Serve the waffles warm with your favorite toppings.

Nutritional Info (per serving): Calories: 250 | Fat: 9g | Carbs: 33g | Protein: 9g

WholeGrain Muffins

Prep: 15 mins | Cook: 20 mins | Serves: 12 muffins

Ingredients:
- 1 cup wholewheat flour (US & UK)
- 1/2 cup all-purpose flour (US & UK)
- 1/4 cup rolled oats (US & UK)
- 1/4 cup granulated sugar (US & UK)
- 1 tablespoon baking powder (US & UK)
- 1/2 teaspoon baking soda (US & UK)
- 1/2 teaspoon salt (US & UK)
- 1 cup milk (US & UK)
- 1/4 cup unsweetened applesauce (US & UK)
- 1/4 cup olive oil (US & UK)
- 1 egg (US & UK)
- 1 teaspoon vanilla extract (US & UK)

Instructions:
1. Preheat your air fryer to 350°F (180°C) for 3 minutes. [Function used: Preheat]
2. In a large bowl, combine wholewheat flour, all-purpose flour, rolled oats, granulated sugar, baking powder, baking soda, and salt.
3. In another bowl, whisk together milk, applesauce, olive oil, egg, and vanilla extract.
4. Pour the wet ingredients into the dry ingredients and stir until just combined.
5. Line a muffin tin with paper liners or lightly grease it.
6. Fill each muffin cup about 2/3 full with the batter.
7. Place the muffin tin in the air fryer basket and air fry for 1820 minutes until the muffins are golden brown and a toothpick insertedinto the center comes out clean. [Function used: Air frying]
8. Once done, remove the muffins from the air fryer and let them cool in the muffin tin for a few minutes.
9. Transfer the muffins to a wire rack to cool completely before serving.

Nutritional Info (per serving): Calories: 150 | Fat: 5g | Carbs: 22g | Protein: 3g

AirFried Pretzels

Prep: 20 mins | Cook: 10 mins | Serves: 6 pretzels

Ingredients:
- 1 pound pizza dough (US & UK)
- 2 tablespoons baking soda (US & UK)
- 1 egg, beaten (US & UK)
- Coarse salt, for sprinkling (US & UK)

Instructions:
1. Preheat your air fryer to 375°F (190°C) for 3 minutes. [Function used: Preheat]
2. Divide the pizza dough into 6 equal portions.
3. Roll each portion into a rope, about 18 inches long.
4. Twist each rope into a pretzel shape.
5. In a shallow dish, dissolve baking soda in 2 cups of warm water.
6. Dip each pretzel into the baking soda solution, then place them on a parchmentlined tray.
7. Brush the pretzels with beaten egg and sprinkle with coarse salt.
8. Place the pretzels in the air fryer basket, leaving space between each one.
9. Air fry for 810 minutes until the pretzels are golden brown and cooked through. [Function used: Air frying]
10. Once cooked, remove the pretzels from the air fryer and let them cool slightly before serving.

Nutritional Info (per serving): Calories: 200 | Fat: 2g | Carbs: 40g | Protein: 6g

CHAPTER 10: DESSERTS

Baked Apples

Prep: 10 mins | Cook: 20 mins | Serves: 4

Ingredients:
- 4 medium apples, cored (US & UK)
- 2 tablespoons unsalted butter, melted (US & UK)
- 2 tablespoons brown sugar (US & UK)
- 1 teaspoon ground cinnamon (US & UK)
- 1/4 cup chopped walnuts (US & UK)
- 1/4 cup raisins (US & UK)

Instructions:
1. Preheat your air fryer to 375°F (190°C) for 3 minutes. [Function used: Preheat]
2. In a small bowl, mix together melted butter, brown sugar, cinnamon, walnuts, and raisins.
3. Stuff each cored apple with the mixture.
4. Place the stuffed apples in the air fryer basket.
5. Air fry for 1820 minutes until the apples are tender. [Function used: Air frying]
6. Serve warm, optionally topped with a scoop of lowsugar vanilla ice cream.

Nutritional Info (per serving): Calories: 180 | Fat: 7g | Carbs:

AirFried Churros

Prep: 15 mins | Cook: 10 mins | Serves: 4

Ingredients:
- 1 cup water (US & UK)
- 2 tablespoons unsalted butter (US & UK)
- 2 teaspoons granulated sugar (US & UK)
- 1/4 teaspoon salt (US & UK)
- 1 cup all-purpose flour (US & UK)
- 1 egg (US & UK)
- 1/2 teaspoon vanilla extract (US & UK)
- 2 tablespoons granulated sugar mixed with 1 teaspoon ground cinnamon, for coating (US & UK)
- Cooking spray

Instructions:
1. In a saucepan, bring water, butter, sugar, and salt to a boil. Remove from heat.
2. Stir in flour until mixture forms a ball.
3. Add egg and vanilla extract, stirring well until fully incorporated.
4. Transfer dough to a piping bag fitted with a star tip.
5. Preheat your air fryer to 375°F (190°C) for 3 minutes. [Function used: Preheat]
6. Pipe strips of dough into the air fryer basket, cutting them with scissors.
7. Lightly coat churros with cooking spray.
8. Air fry for 810 minutes until golden brown and crispy. [Function used: Air frying]
9. Immediately roll hot churros in cinnamon sugar mixture.
10. Serve warm with chocolate dipping sauce, if desired.

Nutritional Info (per serving): Calories: 220 | Fat: 9g | Carbs: 31g | Protein: 4g

Chocolate Avocado Mousse

Prep: 10 mins | Cook: 0 mins | Serves: 2

Ingredients:
- ✓ 1 ripe avocado, peeled and pitted (US & UK)
- ✓ 1/4 cup unsweetened cocoa powder (US & UK)
- ✓ 1/4 cup unsweetened almond milk (US & UK)
- ✓ 2 tablespoons honey or maple syrup (US & UK)
- ✓ 1/2 teaspoon vanilla extract (US & UK)
- ✓ Pinch of salt (US & UK)
- ✓ Fresh berries, for garnish (optional) (US & UK)

Instructions:
1. In a food processor, combine avocado, cocoa powder, almond milk, honey or maple syrup, vanilla extract, and salt.
2. Blend until smooth and creamy, scraping down the sides as needed.
3. Divide mousse into serving glasses.
4. Refrigerate for at least 30 minutes to chill.
5. Serve topped with fresh berries, if desired.

Nutritional Info (per serving): Calories: 200 | Fat: 12g | Carbs: 24g | Protein: 4g

Raspberry Parfaits

Prep: 10 mins | Cook: 0 mins | Serves: 2

Ingredients:
- ✓ 1 cup Greek yogurt (US & UK)
- ✓ 1/2 cup fresh raspberries (US & UK)
- ✓ 2 tablespoons sugarfree granola (US & UK)
- ✓ 1 tablespoon chopped nuts (such as almonds or walnuts) (US & UK)
- ✓ 1 tablespoon honey or maple syrup (optional) (US & UK)

Instructions:
1. In two serving glasses, layer Greek yogurt, fresh raspberries, and sugarfree granola alternately.
2. Repeat the layers until the glasses are filled.
3. Top each parfait with chopped nuts.
4. Drizzle with honey or maple syrup, if desired, for added sweetness.
5. Serve immediately or refrigerate until ready to serve.

Nutritional Info (per serving): Calories: 180 | Fat: 6g | Carbs: 20g | Protein: 14g

Lemon Bars

Prep: 15 mins | Cook: 25 mins | Serves: 9 bars

Ingredients:

For the crust:
- 1 cup almond flour (US & UK)
- 2 tablespoons coconut flour (US & UK)
- 2 tablespoons granulated erythritol or sweetener of choice (US & UK)
- 3 tablespoons unsalted butter, melted (US & UK)

For the filling:
- 2 large eggs (US & UK)
- 1/2 cup fresh lemon juice (US & UK)
- Zest of 1 lemon (US & UK)
- 1/3 cup granulated erythritol or sweetener of choice (US & UK)
- 2 tablespoons almond flour (US & UK)
- 1/2 teaspoon baking powder (US & UK)
- Powdered erythritol, for dusting (optional) (US & UK)

Instructions:
1. Preheat your air fryer to 325°F (160°C) for 3 minutes. [Function used: Preheat]
2. In a mixing bowl, combine almond flour, coconut flour, granulated erythritol, and melted butter to form the crust mixture.
3. Press the crust mixture evenly into the bottom of an 8x8inch baking dish lined with parchment paper.
4. In another bowl, whisk together eggs, lemon juice, lemon zest, granulated erythritol, almond flour, and baking powder until smooth.
5. Pour the lemon mixture over the crust.
6. Place the baking dish in the air fryer basket.
7. Air fry for 2025 minutes until the filling is set and the edges are lightly browned. [Function used: Air frying]
8. Allow the bars to cool completely in the baking dish before slicing.
9. Optionally, dust the bars with powdered erythritol before serving.
10. Slice into squares and serve chilled or at room temperature.

Nutritional Info (per serving): Calories: 150 | Fat: 12g | Carbs: 6g | Protein: 4g

Peanut Butter Cups

Prep: 15 mins | Cook: 0 mins | Serves: 12 cups

Ingredients:
- 1 cup sugarfree dark chocolate chips (US & UK)
- 1/2 cup creamy peanut butter (US & UK)
- 2 tablespoons powdered erythritol or sweetener of choice (US & UK)
- 1 tablespoon coconut flour (US & UK)
- Sea salt, for garnish (optional) (US & UK)

Instructions:
1. In a microwavesafe bowl, melt the dark chocolate chips in 30second intervals, stirring in between until smooth.
2. In another bowl, mix together creamy peanut butter, powdered erythritol, and coconut flour until well combined.
3. Line a mini muffin tin with paper liners.
4. Spoon a teaspoon of melted chocolate into each muffin cup, spreading it evenly along the bottom and up the sides.
5. Place the muffin tin in the freezer for 5 minutes to set the chocolate.
6. Once set, spoon a teaspoon of peanut butter mixture into each chocolate cup, pressing it down gently.
7. Spoon another teaspoon of melted chocolate over the peanut butter layer, covering it completely.
8. Sprinkle a pinch of sea salt on top of each cup, if desired.
9. Return the muffin tin to the freezer for another 1015 minutes to set the peanut butter cups.
10. Once set, remove the paper liners and serve chilled.

Nutritional Info (per serving): Calories: 150 | Fat: 12g | Carbs: 8g | Protein: 5g

Coconut Macaroons

Prep: 15 mins | Cook: 10 mins | Serves: 12 macaroons

Ingredients:
- 2 cups unsweetened shredded coconut (US & UK)
- 1/2 cup sugarfree condensed milk (US & UK)
- 1 teaspoon vanilla extract (US & UK)
- 1/4 teaspoon salt (US & UK)
- 2 large egg whites (US & UK)
- Sugarfree chocolate chips, for drizzling (optional) (US & UK)

Instructions:
1. Preheat your air fryer to 325°F (160°C) for 3 minutes. [Function used: Preheat]
2. In a mixing bowl, combine shredded coconut, sugarfree condensed milk, vanilla extract, and salt.
3. In a separate bowl, beat egg whites until stiff peaks form.
4. Gently fold the beaten egg whites into the coconut mixture until well combined.
5. Using a cookie scoop or spoon, drop rounded tablespoons of the mixture onto a parchmentlined air fryer basket.
6. Place the basket in the air fryer and bake for 810 minutes until the macaroons are lightly golden on top. [Function used: Air frying]
7. Allow the macaroons to cool slightly before drizzling with melted sugarfree chocolate, if desired.
8. Let the chocolate set before serving.

Nutritional Info (per serving): Calories: 120 | Fat: 10g | Carbs: 5g | Protein: 3g

AirFried Fruit Crisps

Prep: 10 mins | Cook: 15 mins | Serves: 4

Ingredients:
- 2 cups mixed fresh fruit (such as apples, peaches, or berries), sliced (US & UK)
- 1 tablespoon lemon juice (US & UK)
- 2 tablespoons granulated erythritol or sweetener of choice (US & UK)
- 1/2 teaspoon ground cinnamon (US & UK)
- 1/4 cup rolled oats (US & UK)
- 2 tablespoons almond flour (US & UK)
- 2 tablespoons chopped nuts (such as almonds or walnuts) (US & UK)
- 1 tablespoon unsalted butter, melted (US & UK)

Instructions:
1. Preheat your air fryer to 375°F (190°C) for 3 minutes. [Function used: Preheat]
2. In a mixing bowl, toss the sliced fruit with lemon juice, granulated erythritol, and ground cinnamon until well coated.
3. Divide the fruit mixture evenly among individual ramekins or ovensafe dishes.
4. In another bowl, combine rolled oats, almond flour, chopped nuts, and melted butter to make the crisp topping.
5. Sprinkle the crisp topping over the fruit in each ramekin, covering it completely.
6. Place the ramekins in the air fryer basket.
7. Air fry for 1215 minutes until the fruit is bubbling and the topping is golden brown and crispy. [Function used: Air frying]
8. Remove the fruit crisps from the air fryer and let them cool slightly before serving.
9. Serve warm, optionally topped with a dollop of whipped cream or a scoop of vanilla ice cream.

Nutritional Info (per serving): Calories: 150 | Fat: 8g | Carbs: 18g | Protein: 3g

Dark Chocolate Bark

Prep: 10 mins | Cook: 0 mins | Serves: 8

Ingredients:
- ✓ 4 ounces sugarfree dark chocolate, chopped (US & UK)
- ✓ 2 tablespoons unsweetened shredded coconut (US & UK)
- ✓ 2 tablespoons chopped nuts (such as almonds or walnuts) (US & UK)
- ✓ 2 tablespoons dried cranberries or other dried fruit (optional) (US & UK)
- ✓ Pinch of sea salt (US & UK)

Instructions:
1. In a microwavesafe bowl, melt the dark chocolate in 30second intervals, stirring in between until smooth.
2. Line a baking sheet with parchment paper.
3. Pour the melted chocolate onto the prepared baking sheet, spreading it into an even layer with a spatula.
4. Sprinkle shredded coconut, chopped nuts, dried cranberries, and a pinch of sea salt over the melted chocolate.
5. Place the baking sheet in the refrigerator for 2030 minutes until the chocolate is set.
6. Once set, break the chocolate bark into pieces.
7. Store in an airtight container in the refrigerator until ready to serve.

Nutritional Info (per serving): Calories: 120 | Fat: 10g | Carbs: 6g | Protein: 2g

Pumpkin Spice Squares

Prep: 15 mins | Cook: 25 mins | Serves: 9 squares

Ingredients:
- For the squares:
- 1 cup almond flour (US & UK)
- 1/4 cup coconut flour (US & UK) AND 1/4 teaspoon salt (US & UK)
- 1 teaspoon baking powder (US & UK)
- 1 teaspoon ground cinnamon (US & UK)
- 1/2 teaspoon ground nutmeg (US & UK)
- 1/4 teaspoon ground ginger (US & UK)
- 1/4 teaspoon ground cloves (US & UK)
- 1/2 cup pumpkin puree (US & UK)
- 1/4 cup coconut oil, melted (US & UK) & 2 large eggs (US & UK)
- 1/4 cup maple syrup or honey (US & UK)

For the glaze:
- 1/2 cup powdered erythritol or powdered sugar (US & UK)
- 12 tablespoons unsweetened almond milk or milk of choice (US & UK)
- 1/4 teaspoon vanilla extract (US & UK)

Instructions:

Preheat your air fryer to 325°F (160°C) for 3 minutes. [Function used: Preheat]

In a mixing bowl, whisk together almond flour, coconut flour, baking powder, cinnamon, nutmeg, ginger, cloves, and salt.

In another bowl, mix pumpkin puree, melted coconut oil, maple syrup or honey, and eggs until well combined.

Gradually add the dry ingredients to the wet ingredients, stirring until a smooth batter forms.

Pour the batter into a greased 8x8inch baking dish lined with parchment paper.

Place the baking dish in the air fryer basket.

Air fry for 2025 minutes until the pumpkin squares are set and lightly golden on top. [Function used: Air frying]

Remove the baking dish from the air fryer and let the squares cool completely.

In a small bowl, whisk together powdered erythritol or powdered sugar, almond milk, and vanilla extract to make the glaze.

Drizzle the glaze over the cooled pumpkin squares.

Slice into squares and serve.

Nutritional Info (per serving): Calories: 180 | Fat: 12g | Carbs: 14g | Protein: 4g

Almond Flour Brownies

Prep: 15 mins | Cook: 25 mins | Serves: 9 brownies

Ingredients:
- 1/2 cup unsalted butter, melted (US & UK)
- 3/4 cup sugarfree sweetener (such as erythritol or stevia) (US & UK)
- 2 large eggs (US & UK)
- 1 teaspoon vanilla extract (US & UK)
- 1 cup almond flour (US & UK)
- 1/4 cup cocoa powder (US & UK)
- 1/2 teaspoon baking powder (US & UK)
- 1/4 teaspoon salt (US & UK)
- 1/4 cup sugar free chocolate chips (US & UK)

Instructions:
1. Preheat your air fryer to 325°F (160°C) for 3 minutes. [Function used: Preheat]
2. In a mixing bowl, whisk together melted butter and sugarfree sweetener until well combined.
3. Add eggs and vanilla extract, and whisk until smooth.
4. In another bowl, sift together almond flour, cocoa powder, baking powder, and salt.
5. Gradually add the dry ingredients to the wet ingredients, stirring until just combined.
6. Fold in sugarfree chocolate chips.
7. Pour the batter into a greased 8x8inch baking dish lined with parchment paper.
8. Place the baking dish in the air fryer basket.
9. Air fry for 2025 minutes until the brownies are set around the edges and slightly firm to the touch. [Function used: Air frying]
10. Remove the baking dish from the air fryer and let the brownies cool completely before slicing into squares.
11. Serve and enjoy!

Nutritional Info (per serving): Calories: 180 | Fat: 15g | Carbs: 8g | Protein: 4g

Strawberry Chia Pudding

Prep: 10 mins (+ chilling time) | Cook: 0 mins | Serves: 2
Ingredients:
- 1 cup unsweetened almond milk (US & UK)
- 1 tablespoon sugar free sweetener (such as erythritol or stevia) (US & UK)
- 1/2 teaspoon vanilla extract (US & UK) AND 1/4 cup chia seeds (US & UK)
- 1/2 cup fresh strawberries, chopped (US & UK)

Instructions:
1. In a mixing bowl, whisk together almond milk, chia seeds, sugarfree sweetener, and vanilla extract until well combined.
2. Let the mixture sit for 5 minutes, then whisk again to prevent clumps.
3. Cover the bowl and refrigerate for at least 2 hours or overnight, until the chia pudding thickens.
4. Once the pudding is thickened, stir in chopped strawberries.
5. Divide the strawberry chia pudding into serving glasses or bowls.
6. Serve chilled and enjoy!

Nutritional Info (per serving): Calories: 120 | Fat: 7g | Carbs: 10g | Protein: 5g

Baked Pears with Honey and Walnuts

Prep: 10 mins | Cook: 15 mins | Serves: 2
Ingredients:
- 2 ripe pears, halved and cored (US & UK)
- 1 tablespoon unsalted butter, melted (US & UK)
- 1 tablespoon honey (or sugarfree syrup for a lowercarb option) (US & UK)
- 2 tablespoons chopped walnuts (US & UK)
- 1/4 teaspoon ground cinnamon (US & UK) AND Pinch of salt (US & UK

Instructions:
1. Preheat your air fryer to 350°F (175°C) for 3 minutes. [Function used: Preheat]
2. In a small bowl, mix melted butter, honey, chopped walnuts, ground cinnamon, and a pinch of salt.
3. Place the pear halves, cut side up, in the air fryer basket.
4. Spoon the honey and walnut mixture evenly over the pear halves.
5. Place the basket in the air fryer and bake for 1215 minutes until the pears are tender and caramelized. [Function used: Air frying]
6. Remove the baked pears from the air fryer and let them cool slightly.
7. Serve the baked pears warm, optionally topped with a dollop of Greek yogurt or a sprinkle of additional cinnamon.

Nutritional Info (per serving): Calories: 150 | Fat: 8g | Carbs: 20g | Protein: 2g

Coconut Flour Cookies

Prep: 15 mins | Cook: 12 mins | Serves: 12 cookies

Ingredients:
- 1/4 cup coconut flour (US & UK)
- 1/4 cup sugarfree sweetener (such as erythritol or stevia) (US & UK)
- 1/4 teaspoon baking powder (US & UK)
- Pinch of salt (US & UK)
- 2 tablespoons unsalted butter, melted (US & UK)
- 1 large egg (US & UK)
- 1/2 teaspoon vanilla extract (US & UK)
- 2 tablespoons unsweetened shredded coconut (US & UK)
- 2 tablespoons sugarfree chocolate chips (US & UK)

Instructions:
1. Preheat your air fryer to 325°F (160°C) for 3 minutes. [Function used: Preheat]
2. In a mixing bowl, whisk together coconut flour, sugarfree sweetener, baking powder, and salt.
3. Add melted butter, egg, and vanilla extract to the dry ingredients, and mix until a dough forms.
4. Fold in shredded coconut and sugarfree chocolate chips.
5. Divide the dough into 12 equal portions and roll each portion into a ball.
6. Place the cookie dough balls on a parchmentlined air fryer basket, spacing them apart.
7. Flatten each cookie slightly with the palm of your hand.
8. Place the basket in the air fryer and bake for 1012 minutes until the cookies are golden brown and set. [Function used: Air frying]
9. Remove the cookies from the air fryer and let them cool on a wire rack before serving.
10. Enjoy these delicious coconut flour cookies!

Nutritional Info (per serving): Calories: 60 | Fat: 4g | Carbs: 4g | Protein: 1g

Carrot Cake Cupcakes

Prep: 20 mins | Cook: 18 mins | Serves: 12 cupcakes

Ingredients:

For the cupcakes:
- 1 cup almond flour (US & UK) & 1 teaspoon baking powder (US & UK)
- 1/4 cup coconut flour (US & UK) & 1/2 teaspoon baking soda (US & UK)
- 1/2 teaspoon ground cinnamon (US & UK) & 1 teaspoon vanilla extract (US & UK)
- 1/4 teaspoon ground nutmeg (US & UK) & 1/4 teaspoon ground ginger (US & UK)
- Pinch of salt (US & UK) & 3 large eggs (US & UK)
- 1/2 cup unsweetened applesauce (US & UK)
- 1/4 cup coconut oil, melted (US & UK) & 1 cup grated carrots (US & UK)
- 1/4 cup sugarfree sweetener (such as erythritol or stevia) (US & UK)
- 1/4 cup chopped walnuts (optional) (US & UK)

For the cream cheese frosting:
- 4 oz cream cheese, softened (US & UK)
- 2 tablespoons unsalted butter, softened (US & UK)
- 1/4 cup powdered erythritol or powdered sugar (US & UK)
- 1/2 teaspoon vanilla extract (US & UK)

Instructions:
1. Preheat your air fryer to 325°F (160°C) for 3 minutes. [Function used: Preheat]
2. In a mixing bowl, whisk together almond flour, coconut flour, baking powder, baking soda, cinnamon, nutmeg, ginger, and salt.
3. In another bowl, beat eggs, applesauce, melted coconut oil, sugarfree sweetener, and vanilla extract until well combined.
4. Gradually add the dry ingredients to the wet ingredients, stirring until just combined.
5. Fold in grated carrots and chopped walnuts, if using.
6. Line a muffin tin with cupcake liners and divide the batter evenly among the liners.
7. Place the muffin tin in the air fryer basket.
8. Air fry for 1618 minutes until the cupcakes are golden brown and a toothpick inserted into the center comes out clean. [Function used: Air frying]
9. Remove the cupcakes from the air fryer and let them cool completely on a wire rack.
10. In a mixing bowl, beat softened cream cheese, softened butter, powdered erythritol or powdered sugar, and vanilla extract until smooth to make the cream cheese frosting.
11. Frost the cooled cupcakes with the cream cheese frosting.
12. Serve and enjoy these delicious carrot cake cupcakes!

Nutritional Info (per serving): Calories: 180 | Fat: 14g | Carbs: 8g | Protein: 5g

CHAPTER 11: BEVERAGES

Fresh Fruit Smoothies

Prep: 10 mins | Serves: 2

Ingredients:
- ✓ 1 cup fresh mixed berries (such as strawberries, blueberries, and raspberries) (US & UK)
- ✓ 1 ripe banana, peeled and sliced (US & UK)
- ✓ 1/2 cup plain Greek yogurt (US & UK)
- ✓ 1/2 cup unsweetened almond milk (US & UK)
- ✓ 1 tablespoon honey or sugarfree sweetener (US & UK)
- ✓ Ice cubes, as desired (US & UK)

Instructions:
1. Place mixed berries, sliced banana, Greek yogurt, almond milk, and honey or sugarfree sweetener in a blender.
2. Add ice cubes if desired for a colder smoothie.
3. Blend on high speed until smooth and creamy.
4. Pour the smoothie into glasses and serve immediately.
5. Enjoy this refreshing and nutritious fresh fruit smoothie!

Nutritional Info (per serving): Calories: 150 | Fat: 2g | Carbs: 28g | Protein: 8g

Iced Herbal Teas

Prep: 5 mins | Cook: 0 mins | Serves: 2

Ingredients:
- ✓ 2 herbal tea bags (such as chamomile, peppermint, or hibiscus) (US & UK)
- ✓ 2 cups boiling water (US & UK)
- ✓ Ice cubes, for serving (US & UK)
- ✓ Fresh lemon slices or mint leaves, for garnish (optional) (US & UK)

Instructions:
1. Place herbal tea bags in a heatproof pitcher or container.
2. Pour boiling water over the tea bags and let steep for 510 minutes.
3. Remove the tea bags and discard.
4. Allow the tea to cool to room temperature, then refrigerate until chilled.
5. To serve, fill glasses with ice cubes and pour the chilled herbal tea over the ice.
6. Garnish with fresh lemon slices or mint leaves if desired.
7. Enjoy this refreshing and caffeinefree iced herbal tea!

Nutritional Info (per serving): Calories: 0 | Fat: 0g | Carbs: 0g | Protein: 0g

Infused Waters

Prep: 5 mins (+ chilling time) | Serves: 2

Ingredients:
- ✓ 2 cups cold water (US & UK)
- ✓ Assorted fruits, vegetables, and herbs (such as cucumber, lemon, lime, berries, mint, or basil) (US & UK)
- ✓ Ice cubes, for serving (US & UK)

Instructions:
1. Fill a pitcher or large jar with cold water.
2. Add your choice of sliced fruits, vegetables, and herbs to the water.
3. Stir gently to combine.
4. Cover the pitcher or jar and refrigerate for at least 1 hour to allow the flavors to infuse.
5. Serve the infused water over ice cubes in glasses.
6. Enjoy this hydrating and refreshing beverage!

Nutritional Info (per serving): Calories: 0 | Fat: 0g | Carbs: 0g | Protein: 0g

Hot Chocolate (Sugarfree)

Prep: 5 mins | Cook: 5 mins | Serves: 2

Ingredients:
- ✓ 2 cups unsweetened almond milk (US & UK)
- ✓ 2 tablespoons unsweetened cocoa powder (US & UK)
- ✓ 2 tablespoons powdered erythritol or sugarfree sweetener (US & UK)
- ✓ 1/2 teaspoon vanilla extract (US & UK)
- ✓ Pinch of salt (US & UK)
- ✓ Sugarfree whipped cream or marshmallows, for serving (optional) (US & UK)

Instructions:
1. In a saucepan, heat almond milk over medium heat until warm but not boiling.
2. Whisk in cocoa powder, powdered erythritol or sugarfree sweetener, vanilla extract, and a pinch of salt until fully combined.
3. Continue to heat the mixture, stirring frequently, until hot but not boiling.
4. Pour the hot chocolate into mugs.
5. Top with sugarfree whipped cream or marshmallows if desired.
6. Enjoy this cozy and guiltfree sugarfree hot chocolate!

Nutritional Info (per serving): Calories: 30 | Fat: 2g | Carbs: 3g | Protein: 1g

Iced Coffee (Unsweetened)

Prep: 5 mins | Serves: 1

Ingredients:
- ✓ 1 cup brewed coffee, chilled (US & UK)
- ✓ Ice cubes (US & UK)

Instructions:
1. Fill a glass with ice cubes.
2. Pour chilled brewed coffee over the ice.
3. Stir gently to combine.
4. Serve immediately and enjoy this refreshing unsweetened iced coffee!

Nutritional Info (per serving): Calories: 0 | Fat: 0g | Carbs: 0g | Protein: 0g

Vegetable Juices

Prep: 10 mins | Cook: 0 mins | Serves: 6. Vegetable Juices

Ingredients:
- ✓ Assorted vegetables such as carrots, cucumbers, celery, spinach, kale, and beets (US & UK)

Instructions:
1. Wash and prepare the vegetables by cutting them into smaller pieces that will fit into your juicer chute.
2. Feed the vegetables through a juicer according to the manufacturer's instructions.
3. Once all the vegetables have been juiced, stir the juice to combine.
4. Pour the vegetable juice into glasses.
5. Serve immediately over ice if desired.
6. Enjoy this nutritious and refreshing vegetable juice!

Nutritional Info (per serving): Calories: Varies depending on vegetables used | Fat: Varies | Carbs: Varies | Protein: Varies

Golden Milk (Turmeric Latte)

Prep: 5 mins | Cook: 5 mins | Serves: 2
Ingredients:
- 2 cups unsweetened almond milk (US & UK)
- 1 teaspoon ground turmeric (US & UK)
- 1/2 teaspoon ground cinnamon (US & UK)
- 1/4 teaspoon ground ginger (US & UK)
- Pinch of ground black pepper (US & UK)
- 1 tablespoon honey or sugarfree sweetener (US & UK)
- 1/2 teaspoon vanilla extract (US & UK)

Instructions:
1. In a small saucepan, combine almond milk, ground turmeric, ground cinnamon, ground ginger, black pepper, honey or sugarfree sweetener, and vanilla extract.
2. Whisk the ingredients together until well combined.
3. Heat the mixture over medium heat, stirring frequently, until hot but not boiling.
4. Once heated through, pour the golden milk into mugs.
5. Serve immediately and enjoy this comforting and antioxidantrich turmeric latte!

Nutritional Info (per serving): Calories: 60 | Fat: 2g | Carbs: 9g | Protein: 1g

Matcha Latte

Prep: 5 mins | Cook: 5 mins | Serves: 2
Ingredients:
- 2 teaspoons matcha powder (US & UK)
- 2 cups unsweetened almond milk (US & UK)
- 1 tablespoon honey or sugarfree sweetener (US & UK)
- 1/2 teaspoon vanilla extract (US & UK)

Instructions:
1. In a small saucepan, whisk together matcha powder and a small amount of almond milk to form a smooth paste.
2. Gradually whisk in the remaining almond milk until fully combined.
3. Add honey or sugarfree sweetener and vanilla extract to the saucepan.
4. Heat the mixture over medium heat, stirring frequently, until hot but not boiling.
5. Once heated through, pour the matcha latte into mugs.
6. Serve immediately and enjoy this energizing and antioxidantpacked matcha latte!

Nutritional Info (per serving): Calories: 60 | Fat: 2g | Carbs: 9g | Protein: 1g

Ginger Tea

Prep: 5 mins | Cook: 10 mins | Serves: 2

Ingredients:
- 2 cups water (US & UK)
- 1inch piece of fresh ginger, thinly sliced (US & UK)
- 1 tablespoon honey or sugarfree sweetener (US & UK)
- 1 tablespoon lemon juice (US & UK)

Instructions:
1. In a small saucepan, bring water to a boil.
2. Add thinly sliced ginger to the boiling water.
3. Reduce heat to low and simmer for 10 minutes.
4. Remove the saucepan from heat and let the ginger steep in the water for an additional 5 minutes.
5. Strain the ginger tea into mugs, discarding the ginger slices.
6. Stir in honey or sugarfree sweetener and lemon juice.
7. Serve immediately and enjoy this soothing and digestive ginger tea!

Nutritional Info (per serving): Calories: 30 | Fat: 0g | Carbs: 8g | Protein: 0g

Chia Fresca

Prep: 5 mins (+ chilling time) | Serves: 2

Ingredients:
- 2 cups water (US & UK)
- 2 tablespoons chia seeds (US & UK)
- 1 tablespoon honey or sugarfree sweetener (US & UK)
- 1 tablespoon lime or lemon juice (US & UK)
- Pinch of salt (US & UK)

Instructions:
1. In a glass jar or bottle, combine water, chia seeds, honey or sugarfree sweetener, lime or lemon juice, and a pinch of salt.
2. Seal the jar or bottle tightly and shake well to combine.
3. Refrigerate the chia fresca for at least 1 hour to allow the chia seeds to swell and thicken the drink.
4. Shake the jar or bottle again before serving.
5. Pour the chia fresca into glasses and serve chilled.
6. Enjoy this refreshing and hydrating chia seed beverage!

Nutritional Info (per serving): Calories: 60 | Fat: 3g | Carbs: 9g | Protein: 2g

Kombucha

Prep: 5 mins | Fermentation: 7-14 days | Serves: Varies

Ingredients:
- 4 cups filtered water (US & UK)
- 4 tea bags (black, green, or a combination) (US & UK)
- 1 cup white sugar (US & UK)
- SCOBY (symbiotic culture of bacteria and yeast) (US & UK)
- 1 cup plain store bought kombucha (US & UK)

Instructions:
1. Boil 4 cups of filtered water in a pot.
2. Remove the pot from heat and add the tea bags and sugar. Stir until the sugar dissolves.
3. Let the tea steep for about 15 minutes, then remove the tea bags and allow the mixture to cool to room temperature.
4. Transfer the cooled tea to a glass jar and add the store-bought kombucha.
5. Gently place the SCOBY on top of the tea mixture.
6. Cover the jar with a clean cloth and secure it with a rubber band.
7. Place the jar in a warm, dark place (around 75-85°F or 24-29°C) for 7-14 days, depending on your desired level of fermentation.
8. After the desired fermentation time, taste the kombucha. It should be slightly tangy with a hint of sweetness.
9. Once fermented to your liking, remove the SCOBY and 1 cup of the kombucha to use as a starter for your next batch.
10. Transfer the remaining kombucha to airtight bottles and refrigerate to stop the fermentation process.
11. Serve chilled and enjoy this homemade, probiotic rich beverage!

Nutritional Info (per serving): Calories: Varies depending on fermentation time | Fat: 0g | Carbs: Varies | Protein: 0g

Kefir Smoothies

Prep: 5 mins | Serves: 2

Ingredients:
- 1 cup plain kefir (US & UK)
- 1 ripe banana (US & UK)
- 1 cup mixed berries (such as strawberries, blueberries, and raspberries) (US & UK)
- 1 tablespoon honey or sugarfree sweetener (US & UK)
- Ice cubes (US & UK)

Instructions:
1. In a blender, combine plain kefir, ripe banana, mixed berries, and honey or sugarfree sweetener.
2. Add ice cubes as desired for a colder smoothie.
3. Blend on high speed until smooth and creamy.
4. Pour the kefir smoothie into glasses and serve immediately.
5. Enjoy this probioticpacked and refreshing kefir smoothie!

Nutritional Info (per serving): Calories: 120 | Fat: 2g | Carbs: 25g | Protein: 5g

Cucumber Mint Water

Prep: 5 mins (+ chilling time) | Serves: 2

Ingredients:
- 2 cups cold water (US & UK)
- 1/2 cucumber, thinly sliced (US & UK)
- 1/4 cup fresh mint leaves (US & UK)
- Ice cubes (US & UK)

Instructions
1. In a pitcher, combine cold water, thinly sliced cucumber, and fresh mint leaves.
2. Stir gently to combine.
3. Cover the pitcher and refrigerate for at least 1 hour to allow the flavors to infuse.
4. Serve the cucumbermint water over ice cubes in glasses.
5. Enjoy this hydrating and refreshing infused water!

Nutritional Info (per serving): Calories: 0 | Fat: 0g | Carbs: 0g | Protein: 0g

Pomegranate Iced Tea

Prep: 10 mins (+ chilling time) | Serves: 2
Ingredients:
- 2 cups water (US & UK)
- 2 black tea bags (US & UK)
- 1/2 cup pomegranate juice (US & UK)
- 2 tablespoons honey or sugarfree sweetener (US & UK)
- Ice cubes (US & UK)
- Fresh pomegranate arils, for garnish (optional) (US & UK)

Instructions:
1. In a small saucepan, bring water to a boil.
2. Add black tea bags to the boiling water and let steep for 5 minutes.
3. Remove the tea bags and stir in pomegranate juice and honey or sugarfree sweetener until fully dissolved.
4. Let the tea mixture cool to room temperature, then refrigerate until chilled.
5. To serve, fill glasses with ice cubes and pour the chilled pomegranate iced tea over the ice.
6. Garnish with fresh pomegranate arils if desired.
7. Enjoy this fruity and antioxidantrich pomegranate iced tea!

Nutritional Info (per serving): Calories: 60 | Fat: 0g | Carbs: 15g | Protein: 0g

Beet Lemonade

Prep: 10 mins (+ chilling time) | Serves: 2
Ingredients:
- 2 cups water (US & UK)
- 1/2 cup beet juice (freshly squeezed or storebought) (US & UK)
- 1/4 cup fresh lemon juice (US & UK) & Ice cubes (US & UK)
- 2 tablespoons honey or sugarfree sweetener (US & UK)
- Fresh mint leaves, for garnish (optional) (US & UK)

Instructions:
1. In a pitcher, combine water, beet juice, fresh lemon juice, and honey or sugarfree sweetener.
2. Stir until the sweetener is fully dissolved.
3. Cover the pitcher and refrigerate for at least 1 hour to chill and allow the flavors to meld.
4. Serve the beet lemonade over ice cubes in glasses.
5. Garnish with fresh mint leaves if desired.
6. Enjoy this vibrant and refreshing beet lemonade!

Nutritional Info (per serving): Calories: 70 | Fat: 0g | Carbs: 19g | Protein: 0g

GLOSSARY TERMS

1. **Diabetes**: A chronic condition characterized by high levels of sugar (glucose) in the blood, either due to inadequate production of insulin by the pancreas or the body's inability to use insulin effectively.

2. **Air Frying**: A cooking method that uses hot air circulation and a minimal amount of oil to fry foods, producing a crispy texture similar to traditional frying methods but with less oil.

3. **Essential Tools**: Equipment necessary for air frying, such as an air fryer appliance, cooking spray, tongs, and a kitchen thermometer.

4. **Ingredients**: Key components used in diabetic-friendly air frying recipes, including fresh produce, lean proteins, whole grains, and healthy fats.

5. **Safety Precautions**: Measures to ensure safe use of an air fryer, such as avoiding overcrowding the basket, using oven mitts when handling hot trays, and keeping the appliance away from flammable materials.

6. **Maintenance Tips**: Guidelines for cleaning and maintaining an air fryer, such as regularly removing and cleaning the basket and tray, wiping down the exterior with a damp cloth, and checking for signs of wear or damage.

7. **Breakfast Delights**: Morning meal options suitable for diabetics, featuring nutrient-rich ingredients like eggs, whole grains, fruits, and vegetables.

8. **Appetizers and Snacks**: Small bites and finger foods perfect for satisfying cravings between meals, with recipes emphasizing vegetables, legumes, and healthy fats.

9. **Soups and Salads**: Nourishing dishes ideal for lunch or dinner, incorporating hearty vegetables, lean proteins, and flavorful broths or dressings.

10. **Vegetarian Mains**: Meatless entrees packed with protein and fiber from sources like tofu, legumes, grains, and vegetables.

11. **Poultry and Seafood**: Recipes featuring lean proteins like chicken, turkey, and fish, cooked with an air fryer to retain moisture and flavor.

12. **Beef and Pork**: Hearty dishes showcasing beef and pork cuts, seasoned and air-fried for a tender texture and rich taste.

13. **Side Dishes**: Accompaniments to main courses, ranging from roasted vegetables and mashed cauliflower to crispy fries and flavorful rice pilaf.

14. **Breads and Baked Goods**: Homemade baked treats made with whole grains and natural sweeteners, including bread, bagels, muffins, and desserts.

15. **Desserts**: Sweet indulgences crafted with diabetic-friendly ingredients, such as fresh fruit, dark chocolate, nuts, and alternative flours.

16. **Beverages**: Refreshing drinks to complement meals, including smoothies, teas, infused waters, and sugar-free hot beverages.

VOLUME MEASUREMENTS

1. Teaspoon (tsp) = 5 milliliters (ml)

2. Tablespoon (tbsp) = 15 milliliters (ml) = 3 teaspoons

3. Fluid Ounce (fl oz) = 29.5735 milliliters (ml) ≈ 30 milliliters (ml)

4. Cup (c) = 240 milliliters (ml) = 8 fluid ounces (fl oz)

5. Pint (pt) = 473.176 milliliters (ml) ≈ 480 milliliters (ml) = 2 cups

6. Quart (qt) = 946.353 milliliters (ml) ≈ 950 milliliters (ml) = 4 cups = 2 pints

7. Gallon (gal) = 3.78541 liters (L) = 4 quarts

Weight Measurements:

1. Ounce (oz) = 28.3495 grams (g)

2. Pound (lb) = 453.592 grams (g) = 16 ounces (oz)

3. Milligram (mg) = 0.001 gram (g)

4. Kilogram (kg) = 1000 grams (g) ≈ 35.274 ounces (oz) ≈ 2.20462 pounds (lb)

Common Cooking Conversions:

1. 1 cup = 16 tablespoons = 48 teaspoons

2. 1 tablespoon = 3 teaspoons

3. 1 pint = 2 cups = 4 gills

4. 1 quart = 2 pints = 4 cups

5. 1 gallon = 4 quarts = 8 pints = 16 cups

Temperature Conversions:

1. Celsius to Fahrenheit: °F = (°C × 9/5) + 32

2. Fahrenheit to Celsius: °C = (°F - 32) × 5/9

Common Oven Temperature Conversions:

1. 350°F = 177°C

2. 375°F = 190°C

3. 400°F = 204°C

4. 425°F = 218°C

5. 450°F = 232°C

Remember, these conversions are approximate and may vary slightly depending on the specific ingredient or measuring tool used. It's always best to double-check conversions when following a recipe, especially for precision in baking.

CONCLUSION

As you turn the final pages of this "Diabetics Air Fryer Cookbook," you can't help but feel a sense of empowerment and excitement for the culinary journey that lies ahead. This collection of recipes is more than just a compilation of airfried dishes – it's a testament to the power of food in managing diabetes and reclaiming control over your wellbeing.

Throughout these pages, we've explored a world of flavors, textures, and culinary possibilities that defy the notion that living with diabetes means sacrificing taste or satisfaction. The air fryer has proven itself to be a true ally, transforming seemingly indulgent dishes into diabetes friendly masterpieces that nourish both body and soul.

As you've flipped through the chapters, you may have found yourself transported to different corners of the globe, savoring the bold spices of Indian curries, the vibrant flavors of Mediterranean salads, or the comforting warmth of classic American comfort foods – all remained to support your diabetes management goals.

Perhaps you've discovered a newfound appreciation for the versatility of vegetables, marveling at how the air fryer can transform humble produce into crispy, craveable delights. Or maybe you've been delighted by the ability to indulge in classic favorites like chicken parmesan or beef burgers without the guilt or adverse effects on your blood sugar levels.

Beyond the recipes themselves, this cookbook has aimed to empower you with knowledge – knowledge about diabetes, its intricacies, and the crucial role that diet plays in managing this condition. Armed with this understanding, you can approach every meal as an opportunity to nourish your body and take control of your wellbeing.

The air fryer has emerged as a powerful ally in this endeavor, offering a way to enjoy delicious, satisfying meals without compromising your health goals. By harnessing its ability to create crispy textures and concentrate flavors with minimal oil, you can savor the tastes you love while reducing your intake of unhealthy fats and calories.

As you continue your journey with the air fryer, remember to embrace a spirit of creativity and adaptability. Don't be afraid to tweak recipes to suit your personal preferences or dietary needs, or to experiment with new flavor combinations that excite your palate. The air fryer is a canvas upon which you can paint your culinary masterpieces, and the possibilities are truly endless.

ENCOURAGEMENT AND PATHING WORDS

Imagine hosting a dinner party where you wow your guests with a spread of airfried delicacies, each dish bursting with flavor and texture while adhering to your diabetesfriendly principles. Picture yourself packing a picnic basket with airfried goodies, ready to savor a delightful alfresco meal without worrying about the impact on your blood sugar levels.

Beyond the kitchen, this cookbook has the potential to inspire those around you to embrace healthier cooking methods and a more mindful approach to their dietary choices. Share your newfound air frying expertise with loved ones, encouraging them to join you on this journey towards a more balanced and flavorful lifestyle – one that prioritizes both enjoyment and wellbeing.

Remember, managing diabetes is a lifelong journey, but it need not be a burden. With the air fryer by your side and this cookbook as your guide, you have the tools to transform your relationship with food, savoring every bite while nourishing your body and supporting your overall health.

As you close this book and embark on your next culinary adventure, carry with you the knowledge that you are part of a vibrant community of individuals who refuse to let diabetes dictate their enjoyment of life's simple pleasures. Together, we celebrate the power of food to nourish, to comfort, and to bring people together – all while prioritizing our health and wellbeing.

So, embrace the air fryer with open arms, and let it become your trusted companion in the kitchen, ushering in a new era of flavorful, diabetesfriendly cooking. The journey ahead may have its challenges, but with each crispy, delectable bite, you'll be reminded that embracing a healthier lifestyle doesn't mean sacrificing taste or joy.

These recipes are more than just a collection of ingredients and instructions – they are a testament to the power of food to heal, to nourish, and to bring people together. Each dish is a celebration of flavor, crafted with the utmost care and attention to the specific needs of those living with diabetes.

As you savor the crispy goodness of airfried delights, you'll be reminded that managing diabetes is not about deprivation or restriction, but rather about finding balance and nourishment in every meal. These recipes empower you to take control of your wellbeing, one delicious bite at a time.

Here's to countless airfried feasts, shared with loved ones over laughter and good conversation. Here's to rediscovering the pure pleasure of cooking and eating, free from guilt or worry. And here's to living your best life, one delicious, diabetesfriendly meal at a time, fueled by the knowledge that you have the power to take control of your health and savor every moment.

Embrace this cookbook as your guide to a world of culinary possibilities, where managing diabetes becomes not a burden, but a journey of flavor, nourishment, and empowerment. Let the air fryer be your ally, and let every bite be a celebration of your commitment to living well.

Printed in Great Britain
by Amazon